CISTERCIAN STUDIES SERIES: NUMBER SEVENTY-THREE

BESA

THE LIFE OF SHENOUTE

# BESA

# THE LIFE OF

# SHENOUTE

INTRODUCTION, TRANSLATION, and NOTES
*by*
*David N. Bell*

Cistercian Publications
Kalamazoo, Michigan
1983

A translation of the Bohairic text edited by J. Leipoldt and W. E. Crum in *Sinuthii Archimandritae Vita et Opera Omnia* I; *Corpus Scriptorum Christianorum Orientalium* 4 / (Copt. 1) (Paris, 1906).

Available in Europe and Britain from

A. R. Mowbray & Co Ltd
St Thomas House  Becket Street
Oxford OX1 1SJ

Available elsewhere from the publisher

Cistercian Publications
WMU Station
Kalamazoo, Michigan  49008

*Printed in the United States of America*
*Typeset by Gale Akins, Kalamazoo*

Library of Congress Cataloguing-in-Publication Data:

Besa, Abbot of Athripe, 5th cent.
  The life of Shenoute.

  (Cistercian studies series ; no. 73)
  Translation of: Sinuthii archimandritae vita et opera omnia.
  Bibliography: p. 115
  Includes index.
  1. Shenute, Saint, d. 466.   2. Christian saints—Egypt—Biography.   I. Bell, David N., 1943–
II. Title.
BR1720.S48B4713  1983    270.2'092'4  [B]    83-5242
ISBN 0-87907-873-1

'O ghastly glories of saints . . . '

Algernon Charles Swinburne
*Hymn to Proserpine*

# TABLE OF CONTENTS

# SHENOUTE OR THE PITFALLS OF MONASTICISM

*Armand Veilleux*

T HE LIFE OF SHENOUTE is not one of the brightest pages of the history of monasticism. It deserves to be known nevertheless, for in monastic tradition the disconcerting figure of the great Shenoute constitutes a tragic phenomenon that compels us to consider seriously some pitfalls inherent in the monastic institution itself.

How can one explain that a man whom all agree in calling authoritarian, harsh, and violent, and whose spirituality, lacking any mystical dimension, his best specialist (J. Leipoldt) describes as 'christ-less' (*christlose Frömmigkeit*), was able for more than eighty years—he died at the age of 118—to impose his authority on a host of disciples who seem to have reached at one point the startling figure of 2200 monks and 1800 nuns? What motives could have attracted to him those masses of disciples among whom, moreover, movements of revolt against the master's authoritarianism seem at times to have reached an endemic stage? Motivations of a socio-economic character must have played a role, but they were certainly not the only reasons. We believe that a more profound explanation is to be sought in the history of the religious phenomenon throughout the ages. Let us try to situate Shenoute in that much broader context, rather than merely in that of monastic Egypt of the fourth and fifth centuries.

Primitive cultures are overwhelming. The great archetypes by which the collective subconscious expresses itself have a very strong hold on a people whose cohesion and unity are preserved by priests, soothsayers, and sorcerers through a well-structured system of myths, rituals, and moral codes. As long as collective survival is not firmly ensured, there is no place for the elaboration of an individual experience and for the blossoming forth of personal consciousness. Any effort by an individual to pursue a personal journey beyond the framework offered by the surrounding culture is excluded. In the beginning, such an effort would be simply impossible and therefore unthinkable; when it becomes possible it is forbidden; and, finally, when it becomes a temptation for a great number it is severely repressed.

Once begun, however, that evolution is irreversible. A day comes when collective survival is sufficiently ensured to allow toleration of some degree of creative marginality. Then the person emerges. The individual relates not only to the group but to each member of it. Bonds are established between persons, and marriage, for example, becomes a relationship between two persons and no longer only between two clans. Then some individuals personally and consciously live the relationship to the Transcendent which had until then been kept in the collective subconscious. Personal vocations are discerned and mystical experiences are lived. It was at such a cultural and religious breakthrough that Abraham heard the call to leave behind all the security—material, psychological, religious—provided by his immediate environment in order to launch out on a personal journey whose various stages and final step he could not foresee. It was in the same period, in early India, that the *munis* fled to the forests to listen to their *Atman* and to encounter *Brahman,* the principle of Being.

Such individual experiences have an impact on the collective psyche, and a religious movement takes form. The number of those who hear the call and answer it increases. We think of the time of the *rishis* of Vedic India and of the patriarchs and Moses in Israel. A mystical experience develops and the collective memory of it comes to be recorded in traditions, beliefs, and rituals. A religion is born; by assuring a functional role the religious movement becomes a system. By this time a plateau has been reached in the pendulum movement between group spirit and personal creativity, in the tension between the collective and the individual poles. That equilibrium will, generally, last several centuries.

After a few centuries of what gradually becomes a respectable mediocrity, the movement toward a more personal religion manifests itself in personal experiences of a particular intensity, like that of Siddhartha Gautama in India, or of the great prophets in Israel. They are solitary seekers who do not try to gather disciples but are anxious to share their deep spiritual experience with all their people. When communities do form around their experience and teaching, they do so by the somewhat natural grouping of those who share the same experience under their inspiration. In this way the buddhist *Sangha* was born; and in the same way the fellowships of the poor of Yahweh developed in Israel during the exile, as, a little later, did the groups of *hasidîm* among whom there blossomed a spiritual attitude impregnated with mysticism that would serve as a seedbed for early christian asceticism.

On that spiritual movement of the *hasidîm* (or Hassidaeans) a few centuries before Christ, a kind of outgrowth developed called Essenism which expressed itself especially in the monastic community of Qumrân and in the communities of Therapeutes in the *diaspora*. It was an involution rather than an evolution. In reaction to the religious and political compromises of the Hasmonaean dynasty, but also in reaction to the insecurity provoked by the opening up of Late Judaism to various esoteric currents, Essenism was a frantic search for security. These people left society to take refuge in the warm security of a religious system as all-pervading as that of primitive cultures, under the all-present personality of the Teacher of Righteousness.

Gnosticism, at the same epoch a very widespread current of thought throughout the East, and one which reached its peak during the first few centuries of the christian era, was also a movement of withdrawal into a form of collectivism leading to individualism rather than to personal development. The mythological frescoes and the philosophical and theological constructions of the gnostic systems were not lacking in grandeur and beauty. The masters of these various schools—Marcion, Basilides, Valentinus, for example—were brilliant, powerful personages, often more inspiring than the heresiologists who fought against them. It is not surprising that they attracted numerous disciples in search of security. At a time when mankind, especially after the revelation of a personal God in Jesus, was reaching a new awareness of the dignity and inalienable responsibility of the human person, gnosticism appeared as an escape into the past, as a search for security in well-organised systems where all human problems received a simple formulation and a firm answer, both guaranteed by the authority of a master invested with powers from above.

Jesus of Nazareth's message was much more disquieting. He did not elaborate a new mythology and did not propose a new doctrinal system or a new moral code. He simply witnessed to his own human and spiritual experience: he said that he had a Father with whom he established a personal relationship of love, from whom he had received a personal mission, and whose will he made his own. He and his Father were one. And he taught that all of us are called to live the same experience: if we love him and accomplish his commandments his Father will love us, he and his Father will come and make their dwelling in us, and we too will be one with his Father and with him. Everyone is invited to work out the consequences and face the demands which such an experience makes in his own personal life.

Christian monasticism, in spite of marked similarities to that of Qumrân, is actually poles apart from it. And notwithstanding some common concepts it may share with gnosticism, it manifests another world of thought and radically different spiritual attitudes. The first great figures of christian monasticism in Egypt—Antony, Makarios, Amoun, for example—were eminently liberated human beings, deeply in touch with their heart and with God. Out of fidelity to a clearly-heard call, they decided to pursue their spiritual journey beyond all that was offered them by the religious and cultural environment of the Church and society of their time. As much as they were free and intransigent in pursuing their pilgrimage on untrodden paths, they also maintained a profound solidarity with men and women of their time. Their aim was nothing less than a personal encounter with God beyond all human mediations.

They did not remain alone very long. Their example released a similar call in many others. Almost against their will they became guides on the way of solitary spiritual adventure. To no one did they offer ready-made maps for the journey; rather they helped each one invent his own unique path.

With Pachomius something different happened, although always in the same line. Pachomius founded a community and established a rule of life. He understood that if a solitary journey toward the discovery of God's will and the realisation of the unique and inalienable 'name' he has given each person can be accomplished in an anchoretic solitude, it can also be accomplished in a community of brothers who respect and support that maturation. In relation to the surrounding religious 'culture' the cenobitic community constitutes a form of 'sub-culture' where a particular type of experience of God is fostered and supported. The rule that structures the life of that group is conceived as a *way* and not as a limit. The various precepts of that rule are so many signposts along the road. The monk must be constantly listening to the Spirit and to his own heart.

Each form of monasticism has its advantages and its riches, but also its limitations and its pitfalls. The principal pitfall of cenobitism lies in the danger that pressure exercised by the collectivity on the individual can easily overwhelm and paralyse him, and risk hampering the growth of its members instead of fostering it. The cenobitic community fulfills its role of being a growth environment inasmuch as it maintains the proper balance between its various constitutive elements.

It was at this point in the evolution of christian monasticism in Egypt that Shenoute came into the picture. The great *White Monastery* near the town of Akhmîm, where he spent some one hundred years of monastic life, was never a pachomian monastery. Its founder, Pjol, Shenoute's uncle, had simply adopted the rule of the pachomian monasteries, modifying it in many respects, especially in the direction of greater austerity. Shenoute accentuated still more that tendency to exaggeration. With that, we are very far from real pachomian spirituality.

In the case of Shenoute and the monastic movement which he directed and by which he was borne, just as in the cases of Qumrân and of gnosticism, we are confronted with a kind of fall-back. In opposition to a developing community spirit and a greater importance given to personal vocation and its demands, there is manifested an instinctive reaction toward the old, well-structured collectivism, which always remains a temptation to human beings. In a massively insecure society, the strongly structured form of monasticism at the White Monastery and the very strong personality of the 'prophet' Shenoute (for so he is called) provided thousands of Egyptian *fellahîn* with the dose of security they needed to quieten their existential and religious anguish. They did not come seeking—and Shenoute did not offer them—guidance and support to help them walk confidently in the way of a fuller realisation of their personal spiritual self and of their identification with Christ, but rather they were looking for strong authority and a rigorous and detailed rule that would assure their escape from perdition and their eternal salvation.

Pachomius came to know Christianity through experiencing the active charity of a community of Christians, and he found his spiritual food in the Gospel, which he knew by heart. It was in the New Testament that he had discovered his sense of Community. Even without the philosophical jargon of the School of Alexandria he was profoundly mystical. He was a demanding spiritual father, always calling his disciples to further growth, but he also had an understanding of human weakness and was attentive to the laws of spiritual growth. Shenoute, on the other hand, was a force of nature, a volcano in perpetual eruption. Generally leading his troops with a rod, he could also at times forget himself to the point of being meek. (According to the witness of one of his own letters, we know that one of his monks died as a consequence of blows he administered.) He acted as an inspired prophet and founded his teaching on an inspiration received directly from above. Without theological formation, he made himself a hunter of heretics, besides leading armed expeditions to overthrow idols and pagan temples. There was nothing mystical about him, but he had a greatly voluntarist approach to spiritual life. He was also an enemy of studies and science, although he himself had received a good intellectual formation (which is generally the case with all those who throughout monastic history have been opposed to studies by monks; de Rancé is another example).

Shenoute's monasticism, like his religion, was a functional one: a certain number of conditions had to be fulfilled in order to obtain a certain result. Everyone knows that a functional religion never leads to a personal experience of God, but history oftentimes proves that it is the best means for engendering mediocrity. To believe that one is a monk because one lives in a monastery, observes all the precepts of the Rule and has firmly poured himself into the 'monastic' mold is the best means never really to become a monk at all.

Benedict of Nursia was very conscious of this when he observed at the end of his Rule that he had simply indicated a minimum by which to reach a respectable mediocrity; to those who wanted to pursue the journey and to pass beyond what the support of the collective structure could give, he proposed the examples and the teachings of the Elders.

If it is interesting and useful to analyse the case of Shenoute and of his White Monastery, this is because it is far from being an isolated one. Of course, few abbots were at the head of their communities for over eighty years, few also used violence as Shenoute did, and few monasteries were ever as populous as the White Monastery! But it is a fact all the same that if we consider the formal aspect, that is, the type of superiorship exercised by Shenoute, many a Shenoute can be found in monastic history, and his kind is not altogether absent from the contemporary scene. In general they are men who are superior and fascinating in many respects. In the Middle Ages a Bernard of Clairvaux, though without the harshness, had much in common with Shenoute. Think of the crowds of disciples brought back to Clairvaux after each *razzia* in the capitals of Europe, at odds with the tradition of the Elders and with the Rule of Benedict, which insists on the necessity of adequately testing the right intention of the candidates. Think most of all of his zeal against heretics. Although he used different methods, his relentless hounding of Abelard was as violent as Shenoute's actions toward Nestorius.

Providing great psychological security by their skill in formulating simply and solving radically any given problem, the Shenoutes are always very influential in deliberative assemblies. Moreover, the great number of disciples they often attract to the monastery seems to prove the correctness of their approach. But beyond the work of grace, the recruitment of a community depends on various other factors, one of them being the type of equilibrium established within the given community between the various elements of common life.

Saint Benedict defines cenobites as monks who have chosen to live in a community, under a rule and an abbot. The community's equilibrium implies a healthy tension among those three poles: community, rule, and abbot. That equilibrium is difficult to maintain; the tension is demanding and rarely attracts crowds. But as soon as the tension is broken in favour of one of the poles, everything becomes easier and the takers are usually more numerous.

A few decades ago, when a type of democratic spirit was popular, a monastery where the communal and dialogal aspects were strongly stressed had a good chance of attracting many candidates. That period seems to be over. Nowadays, young persons who have grown up in a universe of insecurity (in political, economic, and social life as well as in school and often also in the family) gather more easily where a strong stress is put either on the rule (i.e. a firmly structured life-style), or on the charismatic role of the father or the mother. This corresponds fairly well to a fundamentalist tendency found at all levels of society in the West nowadays. But it is an alarming tendency, for the demarcation line between fundamentalism and fanaticism is very tenuous and very easily crossed—generally in the name of very high ideals.

For many candidates today, the monastery is a port of arrival, where a difficult and at times tormented journey on the stormy sea of the world comes to an end. They contemplate spending their lives in harbour, as in a kind of spiritual refugee camp. They need a White Monastery; and every White Monastery needs its Shenoute. For others, however, the monastery is not a port of arrival but a port of call from which constant expeditions on the high seas are possible (which in no way implies leaving the enclosure of the monastery). It is the place they have chosen for carrying on an ever new journey, a search beyond all institutional mediations toward the encounter with God who is beyond everything that can be said of him and who is other than everything that is taught about him by those who think they can easily speak of him. These pilgrims of the Absolute need to live in communion with other frontier runners, under the guidance of an *higoumenos,* according to the beautiful name given the abbot by an ancient tradition, that is, someone who guides others on the way. Neither a White Monastery nor a Shenoute could answer their spiritual needs.


At every moment of history, religious movements are coming to birth; most of them have an ephemeral existence of a few decades or a few centuries. Monasticism is a trans-cultural phenomenon that has existed for thousands of years. It has been able to survive not only all the crises of society and of the Church, but even its own periods of decadence. Like the phoenix it renews itself. Periodically, after, some-times rather long, phases of larval existence, it recovers the freshness and the dynamism of a butterfly emerging from the cocoon. But much collective discernment is required to be able to recognise in today's chrysalis tomorrow's butterfly; for it is not enough to enter one's cocoon to be borne anew.

Throughout the world, in every culture, in all religions and every walk of life there are nowadays—as much as at any earlier time and probably more than at any earlier time—women and men thirsty for the Absolute, open to the Breath of Life of which Paul speaks in chapter 8 of his Epistle to the Romans, and straining toward that surplus of life, unforesee-able and unimaginable, that is always offered to them from on high. They live in a tent, nomads of the Absolute, frontier runners, always ready to receive under a new form the 'name' that engenders in them their inner being, accepting the various institutional mediations, but refusing to be imprisoned by them. In them, the monastic charism survives, more perhaps than in all the official institutional forms, even if these have been retouched according to Vatican II.

And when the monastic institution itself comes to realise a new phase of growth, as it has done at various times in the past, it will not be through a reform ('adapted' though it be) of its existing structures, but by the regrouping of all these solitary wayfarers, in one form or another, in a sort of great universal monastic order. That network exists already; it has still to invent its visible mode of expression. One must hope that a few elements of that network will then be found in every White Monastery.

Armand Veilleux

*N.-D. de Mistassini*

# INTRODUCTION

IN THE *LAUSIAC HISTORY* of Palladius and the *Conferences* of John Cassian, Shenoute of Atripe makes no appearance. No apophthegms of his are recorded in the *Apophthegmata Patrum*, nor is he to be found in the *Historia monachorum in Aegypto*. Yet some have ranked him second to Pachomius for his contribution to the development of Egyptian monasticism, and his name is still accorded the highest veneration in the Coptic Orthodox Church. Why, then, this curious neglect on the part of these, and other, early writers? The reason is simple: they were, for the most part, Greeks writing for a Hellenistic audience, and Shenoute of Atripe was first and foremost a Copt. His way of thinking was Coptic; his monks and his monastery were Coptic; and all his surviving letters and sermons were written in Coptic. Indeed, it was Shenoute who was primarily responsible for the development of Coptic literature. Before his time, Coptic writing was confined almost entirely to biblical translations from Greek, but Shenoute took the vernacular of his own area, developed it into a rich and flexible idiom, and used it to produce original writings of great vitality and unmistakable character. With the force of his tremendous authority behind it, it was Shenoute's dialect, later to be called Sahidic, which gradually displaced the other dialects and established itself as the standard literary idiom of Christian Egypt until it was itself supplanted by Bohairic in the later middle ages.[1] Shenoute's Coptic is very much his own: it reflects clearly his personality as well as his ideas, and there is no better way to come to an appreciation of his thought and his character than to read what he wrote.[2]

1

It was this very Copticism which doomed Shenoute to oblivion. The Hellenistic inhabitants of Egypt regarded the language much as the Normans in England regarded Anglo-Saxon: it was a poor language fit only for peasants, and no civilized man would bother with it. You might have used it when giving orders to your cook, but you certainly did not speak it with your friends. Greek, whose celestial harmonies soothed the sophisticated ear, was the only language worthy of any civilized being. Shenoute's renown, therefore, was confined within the boundaries of Coptic Egypt. The Greek and Latin writers ignored him, and Greek monasticism owes nothing to him. But to the Copts, to whom he gave so much, he was everything,[3] and the fact that outside Egypt he is so little known is not an indication of his lack of importance, but a reflection of linguistic and cultural prejudice.

It is understandable, therefore, that the *Life of Shenoute* here translated should have been written in Coptic, not in Greek, and that as far as one can tell, no Greek version of it was ever made. The early suggestion of François Nau, that the original *Life* was in Greek and that the Coptic is a translation, has long since been discounted,[4] and there is now no longer any doubt that the *Vita* was an original Coptic production and that it was written by Besa, Shenoute's disciple, friend, and successor.[5] To understand Besa's place in the story, however, we must go back to the middle of the fourth century when an ascetic by the name of Pjol (see n. 11),[6] who was actually the brother of Shenoute's mother (see *Vita* 7[7]), founded the White Monastery hard by the ruins of ancient Atripe in the Theban desert. The site is just a few miles from the modern town of Akhmîm in Upper Egypt (see n. 9).[8] Under the rule of Pjol, the White Monastery (so called because of the colour of its walls) attained what Émile Amélineau referred to as 'an honest mediocrity',[9] and it was to this monastery that Shenoute came as a young boy. In due course, as we shall see a little later, Shenoute succeeded Pjol as abbot (it would seem that this occurred about

385 CE[10]), and under Shenoute's charismatic leadership the White Monastery, never very large during the abbacy of Pjol, attracted thousands of monks and nuns and was transformed into a monastic centre of great size and importance. Here, in turn, came Besa, Shenoute's disciple, who was nominated by Shenoute himself to succeed him as he had previously succeeded Pjol.[11] On Shenoute's death, therefore, which seems to have occurred in 466 CE,[12] Besa found himself abbot of one of the largest monasteries in Egypt, and it was he who, in later years, wrote the life of his holy and esteemed predecessor which is translated in this present volume.

Little is known of Besa's own life. No *Vita* has come down to us, and the few biographical fragments which can be gleaned from his own writings have been admirably summarized for us in the excellent articles of K. H. Kuhn.[13] We do not know the date of his birth, nor that of his death. He seems to have still been alive in 474 CE[14], but his age at that time is unknown. We know nothing of his family or of his background, and we have no clue as to how old he was when he entered the White Monastery. He must have been a capable man—had he not been so, Shenoute would not have named him as his successor—and although he was much gentler and far less ferocious than his formidable predecessor, he appears to have been a conscientious abbot, and was remembered in monastic circles long after his death.[15] His name appears coupled with that of Shenoute in the liturgy of the Coptic Orthodox Church[16], and there is a splendid icon depicting Besa and Shenoute together in the Church of St Shenoute, Dair Abû's-Saîfaîn, in Old Cairo.

Besa's *Life of Shenoute,* as we have noted, was originally written in Sahidic Coptic, the dialect canonized by Shenoute. But of this original Sahidic *Life,* only fragments remain.[17] In the Middle Ages, when Bohairic had superceded Sahidic as the official language of the Coptic church, Besa's *Life* was translated into the latter dialect, and in this form has come to us in a small number of complete manuscripts.[18] The Bohairic text was first edited by Amélineau in the late nineteenth century,[19] and then again in 1906[20] in a much better edition by Johannes Leipoldt and W. E. Crum. It is this last edition which has been used as the basis for the present translation, and the section numbers used here are those which appear in the Leipoldt/Crum text.

The Bohairic *Life* of Besa is not the only *Life* we have. There is an Arabic *Life* which is much longer and more detailed than that of Besa, although it is clearly based on his.[21] It was Amélineau's view that this Arabic *Life* was actually a more faithful rendering of the original Sahidic, and that the Bohairic Life was not only a re-translation of the Sahidic prototype, but also an abridgement of it.[22] This view now has little credence, and all reputable modern scholars see the Arabic *Life* as a later adaptation and elaboration of Besa's original text.[23] Some of its interpolations, in fact, could not have been produced before the late seventh century.[24] This Arabic *Life* provides a large amount of material and a large number of names which are wholly absent from the shorter Bohairic version. We are told, for example, that the names of Shenoute's parents were Darouba and Agbous; that the cantor who accompanied apa Martyrius of Phbōou (see *Vita* 93) was called David; that the brother who sinned and was expelled from the White Monastery (*Vita* 98) was called Shoura; that the brothers who accompanied Shenoute on his iconoclastic expedition to Gesios' house (*Vita* 125 ff.) were called Jusab and Akhnoukh; and so on. We are also told of Shenoute's vigorous asceticism when he was a young man; of how he retired for five years to a cave in the inner desert; of how he crucified himself for a week. And whereas the Bohairic *Life* simply tells us that Shenoute at one time, perhaps in about the year 450 (see n. 66), rescued a number of captives from the Blemmyes, 'brought them to the monastery, provided them with expenses, and sent them away in peace' (*Vita* 90), the

Arabic *Life* informs us that there were twenty thousand such captives, excluding women and children, and that they stayed at the White Monastery for three months. We are then given details as to how Shenoute arranged for physicians and medicines for those who were injured, how many of them died, how many babies were born, the quantity of vegetables, lentils, wheat, oil, and bread, which was necessary to feed them, and the total cost of this exceptionally lavish hospitality.[25] How much reliance can be placed upon these figures is a different matter. The Arabic panegyric certainly enhances the supernatural aspect of Shenoute's life and its author unquestionably exaggerates[26], but this is not to say that his additions and elaborations are purely imaginary. Most studies of Shenoute, for instance, note that under his administration the White Monastery contained some 2200 monks and 1800 nuns, but the only authority for these figures is a single passage in the Arabic *Life*.[27] These numbers, as Leipoldt has demonstrated, are quite reasonable and may well represent an authentic tradition[28], but there is no doubt that we must exercise extreme caution in using such material to construct a history or a biography. The *Lives* of Shenoute, as Amélineau has said, were produced to edify rather than to inform[29], and the quest for the historical Shenoute must be undertaken with no less circumspection than that for the historical Jesus.

The Syriac *Lives* need not long detain us. In 1898 Ignazio Guidi published a fragment of a Syriac *Life* from a manuscript in the British Museum[30], and a year later François Nau published a second Syriac version from a manuscript at present in Paris.[31] Neither of these has much to offer. The former is very close to the Arabic *Life* we have just been discussing, and the latter is a little more than a compilation of selected extracts from the Coptic *Life*. There are certainly interesting questions as to the precise relationship of these Syriac *Lives* to the Arabic and the Coptic—the question, for example, as to whether the Syriac fragments of Guidi derive

from the Arabic or whether the Arabic derives from the
Syriac, or again, whether the Syriac summary of Nau is
based on the Bohairic or whether it represents an inde-
pendent translation of the original Sahidic[32] —but as far as
their content is concerned, and that is our prime interest
here, they offer nothing which cannot be found in greater
detail in the Arabic and the Bohairic.

The Bohairic *Life,* however, despite the fact that it is
certainly closer to the original Sahidic than is the Arabic,
must also be treated with great caution. It falls into the formal pattern for this type of work, and Besa is obviously
more interested in narrating miraculous and marvellous
stories to augment his hero's reputation than in providing
historical data for the use of later scholars. His account is
also quite obviously biased. Besa's Shenoute is a charismatic
wonder-worker with a righteous hatred of heathens and
heretics, and appears on the whole to be a man whom any
orthodox Christian of conservative persuasion might be
happy to serve. Of his more violent actions we hear little,
and what we do hear is subtly disguised (see n. 58). But as we
shall see in due course, Shenoute's violence was all too well
known, having resulted on one occasion in the death of a
monk, and caused him serious problems in later life. We
cannot therefore lay too much emphasis on Besa's *Life* as an
historical or biographical source, and to learn more about
Shenoute and his character we must turn to his own writings.
This approach was taken by Johannes Leipoldt in his
doctoral dissertation on Shenoute completed at Leipzig in
1903 and published in an expanded version later that same
year.[33] This is still the best full-length study of Shenoute
available, and despite the fact that it is now over eighty years
old it yet remains of fundamental importance.[34] It is true
that in certain matters (such as Shenoute's dates) the work
needs revision, and it is equally true that there are now
available to us many more texts than Leipoldt could use, but
the volume was an excellent piece of scholarship for its time,

and in a number of areas—the analysis of Shenoute's character, for example, or the examination of his spirituality, or the investigation of the life and work of the White Monastery— Leipoldt's volume still has a very great deal to offer. Who then was Shenoute of Atripe, what was he really like, and why was he important in the history of Egyptian monasticism?

According to Besa, Shenoute (the name, incidentally, means 'son of God'[35]) was born in the village of Shandawîl near the town of Akhmîm in Upper Egypt (see nn. 7 and 9), but neither the date of his birth nor of his death is known with certainty. Ladeuze suggested that he died in 452[36]; Leipoldt argued for 451[37]; Nau thought sometime before Chalcedon[38]; most modern scholars seem to prefer the arguments of Bethune-Baker who demonstrated that Nestorius survived Chalcedon, Shenoute survived Nestorius, and that his death most probably occurred in 466.[39] According to Besa, Shenoute was one hundred and eighteen years old when he died (see *Vita* 174 ff.)[40], and if this is so, it would require a birth-date of the year 348, just about mid-way through the patriarchate of Athanasius the Great.[41] The problem, of course, is whether we can believe that Shenoute achieved this remarkable age, for Leipoldt has rightly stressed that oriental estimates of longevity are often grossly unreliable.[42] A good example is the case of John of Lycopolis (see n. 79): according to the *Historia monachorum in Aegypto,* he was ninety when he died[43], but Palladius seems to imply that he was only in his seventies.[44] It is true that the way of life of these desert fathers could have transformed their bodies into little more than bone, sinew, and leather, and thereby rendered them virtually indestructible, but whether Shenoute really attained Moses' advanced age (see *Vita* 174) must remain a moot question. He certainly thought he did, and he was certainly very old, but there is little more that we can say.

There is, in fact, only one definite date in the whole life of

our hero: his attendance at the Council of Ephesus in 431
(see *Vita* 128-130). This is confirmed by references in
Shenoute's own writings, and also by the fragments of an important Coptic history of the church which served as a basis
for the later Arabic *History of the Patriarchs of Alexandria*
compiled in the tenth century by Severus/Sawîrus ibn
al-Muqaffa', bishop of El-Ashmûnein.[45] From certain references in a sermon preached in this year, Leipoldt was able to
deduce that Shenoute became a monk in 370 or 371, and
succeeded his uncle Pjol as abbot of the White Monastery in
about 385.[46] This latter date is further supported by certain
remarks in a letter sent from Shenoute to the twenty-second
patriarch of the Alexandrian church, Timothy, who died in
384.[47] If these dates are correct, and there is a very good
chance that they are, and if Shenoute did indeed live to the
formidable age he thought he did, he would have been in his
early twenties when he made his profession. It may seem at
first glance that this conflicts with a passage in the Arabic
*Life* which informs us that Shenoute entered the White
Monastery at the age of nine.[48] In fact, there is no contra-
diction, for if this information is correct, and there is *a
priori* no reason why it should not be, the reference is to
Shenoute's entry into Pjol's cloister as an oblate, and oblates
of tender years were common sights in Coptic monasteries
(see n. 87). Shenoute's parents may have been dead by the
time[49], and if this were the case, the White Monastery would
have been his home, and Pjol would have been a father to
him as well as his uncle and his abbot.

Of Shenoute's early days in the White Monastery we have
little record. The Arabic *Life,* as we have seen, tells us something of his ascetic exercises and of how he retired for five
years to the inner desert, but how much reliance can be
placed on these stories is another matter.[50] Amélineau has
conjectured that he was master of novices under Pjol, but
apart from major problems concerning both the existence
and the nature of the novitiate in fourth-century Egyptian

monasteries, there is no sound evidence for this suggestion.[51] In fact, until Shenoute succeeded Pjol in about 385, his life is wholly obscure, and is marked by little more than those characteristic stories which are used to illustrate singular and precocious sanctity in other similar texts. It may well be true that the boy was accustomed to praying in water-cisterns (see *Vita* 4)—Egypt can boast of stranger things—but we certainly cannot be sure.

On his succession to the abbacy of the White Monastery, Shenoute engineered a transformation. Under Pjol, the monastery had never been large, and the strictness and austerity of Pjol's rule (see n. 11) did little to attract new blood. Shenoute, however, combined strictness and austerity with an amazing charisma, and there can be no doubt that whatever his faults (and they were many) he could attract monks and nuns as a light in the darkness attracts moths. This may seem strange to us when we consider his character, for he was truly a ferocious personality and on many occasions wholly unpredictable. 'Violent', says Leipoldt, is virtually an epithet of Shenoute[52], and Amélineau has characterized him as a man of action, invective, and anathemas.[53] He likens him to an erupting volcano: an impressive sight, though not necessarily a pretty one.[54] He was a self-confident autocrat and a dictator[55], and a man who had no hesitation in inflicting grievous bodily harm on those who transgressed his commands.

Pjol's rule was itself a more rigorous version of the rule of Pachomius, and the rule—or, more precisely, the 'canons' (see n. 70)—of Shenoute were still more severe and much more comprehensive. Shenoute was concerned with the most trivial points—Leipoldt speaks of his 'pedantic conscientiousness'[56]—and considered no part of the running of the monastery and no action of any monk beneath his attention. He demanded of every person who entered the monastery that they sign a covenant, a *diathēkē,* which stipulated the basic minimum for the pursuit of the holy life:

Every person shall say this: I vow before God in

his holy place, the word which I have spoken with
my mouth being my witness: I will not defile my
body in any way; I will not steal; I will not bear
false witness; I will not lie; I will not do anything
deceitful secretly. If I transgress what I have
vowed, I will see the kingdom of heaven, but will
not enter it. God, before whom I made the covenant, will destroy my soul and my body in the
fiery Gehenna because I transgressed the covenant I made.[57]

Any transgressions of this covenant, or any transgressions of
Shenoute's innumerable canons, could be punished with
beatings or with expulsion from the monastery. Such beatings
were severe: in one of his letters Shenoute demands that a
number of delinquent nuns suffer from ten to forty blows,
the blows to be delivered, as was the custom, on the soles of
the feet[58], and there is the famous incident to which we
referred earlier, narrated in one of Shenoute's own letters, of
a monk who died as a result of such a beating.[59] This sort of
discipline was no light tap on the hand, but a bodily assault
of the most determined character, and it is understandable
that there was considerable opposition to it, opposition
which was much greater than later writers (including Besa)
would have us believe.[60] On the other hand, it may again
surprise us that this was not the main reason for the opposition to Shenoute, and that although his violence was, on
occasion, deplored, it was his use of the penalty of expulsion
which caused much greater concern.[61] To comprehend this
we must appreciate the nature of the monks and nuns who
flocked to Shenoute's cloister and understand the place
which such a monastery occupied in the spiritual and
economic life of Christian Egypt.

The great majority of entrants into the White Monastery
both in Shenoute's time and in Besa's came from the
poverty-stricken peasantry, the *fellahîn,* of Upper Egypt[62],
and Shenoute seems to have had a much greater concern for

these people than was customary in his day.[63] The common attitude to the *fellahîn* was that they were more than beasts, but less than men,[64] and they were so accustomed to blows and beatings that Shenoute's violence in implementing his canons was simply the continuation of a long-established tradition. As De Lacy O'Leary observes, 'the stick has been for immemorial ages the means of teaching and ruling the Egyptian fellahîn, and Shenoute was doing no otherwise than every great land-owner and official in the country when he had recourse to corporal chastisement'.[65] According to Leipoldt, the Coptic peasantry was, on the whole, an uneducated slave-people[66], and in the disastrous economic conditions of fourth and fifth century Egypt, many of them lived from hand to mouth, and many of them did not live at all. It is against this background that we may see the importance of the White Monastery, and it is this which enables us to appreciate why expulsion was so much feared.

The characteristic feature of Egyptian coenobitism was work, and the monasteries had developed into highly organized industrial centres. The standard activity was rope and basket making (see n. 75), but we also find weaving and tailoring of linen, cultivation of flax, leather-work and shoe-making, writing and book-binding, and a few carpenters, smiths, and potters.[67] Since the wares, whatever they were, were produced comparatively cheaply, the monks could corner the market in certain important commodities and, as a consequence, the monasteries could become self-sufficient or self-supporting units. In its hey-day, therefore, the White Monastery, with some twenty square miles of land[68] and hundreds of monks and nuns, was a most important economic institution in the region of Akhmîm and, seen as a great industrial cooperative, it enabled thousands of poor *fellahîn* to find both accomodation and employment.[69] The monastic life might have been a life of unremitting labour, but it was much better than starving, and to be expelled from such a monastery and. cast. upon one's own resources

was a very serious matter. Expulsion, therefore, was a punishment of far greater gravity than beating. One of the main
reasons for expulsion was theft, and since theft, unfor-
tunately, was all too common under both Shenoute and Besa,
expulsion was no infrequent matter.[70]

As we said earlier, it was expulsion which provoked the
greatest opposition to Shenoute both in the men's and the
women's cloisters. Some of this opposition was theological
biblical passages were quoted at Shenoute to show that his
intolerance and severity were hardly Christian.[71] Some of it
escalated into out-and-out rebellion. On one occasion at least,
Shenoute was physically attacked[72], and the anti-Shenoute
party appealed to powerful friends in the civil administration
of the area to come to the monastery and do something about
the unwarranted excesses of their terrible abbot. They should
have known better. When the authorities arrived, Shenoute
attacked the magistrate, hurled him to the ground and
trampled on him, and shouted to the other monks to deal
with his fleeing entourage (see n. 58). It was an unmitigated
victory for the abbot of the White Monastery, though, as we
shall see, it was not the only time that Shenoute's behaviour
caused him trouble with the authorities.

Despite the strength of this opposition, it seems that the
supporters of Shenoute were in the majority, and there can be
no doubt this his own personal magnetism had much to do
with this. Leipoldt has pointed out with justice that we cannot
think of Shenoute simply as a pedantic and violent autocrat
and tyrant.[73] Besa's *Life,* despite its formal pattern, indicates
clearly that he and many other monks not only respected Shenoute, but also loved him, and we cannot look merely to economic advantage to explain the thousands of *fellahîn* who
flocked to him and the White Monastery in the second half of
the fourth century and the first half of the fifth. Shenoute was
unquestionably a strange mixture: violent and gentle by turns
(there were times, *mirabile dictu,* when his supporters
accused him of being too lenient![74]), often quite unpredict-

able, but undoubtedly possessed of that indescribable something which separates inexorably the leaders from the led.

His personality is reflected in his language. His Coptic style
is powerful and distinctive, and a considerable amount of
work is being done at present on the peculiar characteristics
and idiosyncrasies of his grammar and his syntax.[75] Words
and thoughts tumble over each other. He can be persuasive
and gentle in one breath, and violent and rude—sometimes
exceedingly rude—in another. He soars masterfully into the
rarefied heights of pure rhetoric and the next moment
descends into colloquial vagueness. We find long sentences
in which the latter part seems to have lost all touch with the
former, and we see his habit of piling on top of each other a
series of words and phrases all of which mean essentially the
same thing.[76] Throughout all this welter of words runs
the Bible. Crum has justly referred to Shenoute's 'endless
quotations' of scripture[77], and it is rare to find an argument
or a polemic in which his case is not supported by a collection of apposite scriptural passages. His memory was astonishing, though when we consider the nature and importance
of 'meditation' or 'recitation' in Coptic monasticism (see
n. 67), it is less astonishing than we may think. 'Meditation'
is required by both the Sinuthian and Pachomian canons[78],
but it does not normally refer to interior silent reflection, the
*meditatio* of the mediaeval west. It usually implies the continual audible repetition of biblical passages learned by heart
(especially passages from the Psalms), and such a practice,
repeated day in and day out, would teach a person the
Scripture whether he wished to be taught or not. This is what
Shenoute's monks were doing when they were visited by
John the Baptist, Elijah, and Elisha (*Vita* 117), and Shenoute
himself could hardly have bettered Pesenthius, who knew by
heart the whole of the Psalter, the twelve minor prophets, and
the gospel of John.[79]

Shenoute's learning, however, was not confined to Scripture. Unlike the vast majority of his monks, he was fluent in

Greek as well as his native Coptic, and was fairly well, though shallowly, acquainted with Greek thought and Greek theology. At the time, there was little bilingualism in the Thebaid, and apart from a few pedagogical tools for Copts who wanted to learn Greek, that language was for the most part restricted to liturgical texts.[80] Greek at the White Monastery, for example, was almost non-existent, but we have a bilingual Greek–Sahidic liturgy which dates from about the time of Shenoute or Besa.[81] Shenoute, however, was an exception: he knew the language well (though where he learned it remains a mystery), he never needed an interpreter, and his writings are liberally sprinkled with multitudes of Greek loan-words which no monoglot Copt living in or around Akhmîm could ever have encountered.[82] Whether his pupil Besa was as linguistically competent remains a disputed question. He seems to have had a smattering of Greek, but he never wrote it and seems never to have spoken it, and we have no clear idea of how much he understood.[83]

Shenoute, then, was certainly bilingual and, as we noted earlier, was also acquainted with Greek ideas. It is clear from his writings that he knew of the Platonic school and was also familiar with some of the Greek legends, though in neither case does he impress us with the depth of his knowledge. He refers in passing to Platonism simply to condemn it, and he mentions the Greek myths only to ridicule them.[84] The case of his allusion to the works of Aristophanes is also less impressive than it may appear. In 1894 Adolf Erman recognized that in one of his invectives against the pagans Shenoute quoted two fragments of Aristophanes, one from the *Birds* and one from the *Frogs,* and proposed that he could have become acquainted with the work of the Greek comedian by attending a performance of the plays while at Ephesus in 431.[85] Ursula Treu has suggested that this is infinitely unlikely. She has the greatest difficulty in visualising Shenoute at a performance of Aristophanes, and points out that if, in fact, he was familiar with his work, he need not have attended his plays to have become so. Papyri of Aristophanes dating from the fourth and fifth centuries were not unknown in Egypt, and there are many citations of the playwright in the Greek literature of the period. Nevertheless, she continues, a close examination of Shenouté's reference does little to convince us that he had really read his sources, and Treu suggests that it is much more likely that he had come across the passage in the apologetic of one of the Greek fathers of the church.[86]

In the case of Aristotle we are on firmer ground. There is sound evidence to show that Shenoute was familair with parts of his *Physiologus*[87], but it is also true that he need not have read Greek to have attained such familiarity. There were certainly translations of the text in Syriac, Ethiopic, and Arabic, and the work of van Lantschoot has demonstrated clearly the very high probability of a Coptic translation as well.[88] It was a popular and widely-distributed treatise, and Shenoute's acquaintance with it should come as no surprise.

Of the christian fathers, our author had certainly read some of Athanasius—the *Life of Antony* and certain of the homiletical works—and he knew the letters of Antony, some of the letters of Pachomius, and, in all probability, some of the work of Evagrius.[89] He mentions Origen, whom he recognised as heretical, and he was also acquainted with certain non-canonical texts which enjoyed a fairly wide circulation among Christians of the time: the *Acts of Archelaus* and the *Gospel of Thomas*.[90] Nevertheless, we must not think of him as a profound and original thinker, a man who read deeply in the Greek fathers and distilled from them his own sagacious doctrines. It is true that the publication by Lefort in 1955 of the 'christological catechesis' attributed to our author has forced us to revise somewhat our opinion of his theological competence[91], but it has not, in my own view, forced us to revise it much. Here, as elsewhere, Shenoute misunderstood Nestorius—a matter we shall discuss further in a moment—and a careful reading of this document does little to persuade us that we are here dealing with a 'well-informed and original' theologian.[92] Shenoute himself made it clear that he had no time for learning. If it is not impossible (for if you do not know the way of a ship on the sea or the way of an eagle in the sky, how can you know the mysteries of God?[93]), it is unprofitable.[94] He would have agreed with the Buddha, with whom he had more than this in common, that there was a multitude of questions which did not tend to enlightenment. His own learning was wide, but rather shallow. He never really appreciated the *esprit* of the Greek theologians, and his understanding of the essential points in the theological controversies of his times left much to be desired.

Why, then, did Cyril of Alexandria take him to Ephesus? It was not for his undoubted eloquence—Cyril was eloquent enough himself—and it was most unlikely to have been for his theological expertise. Leipoldt has suggested that Cyril took Shenoute with him as a bodyguard[95], and given the apa's tendency to violent and aggressive action, this is not wholly impossible. Cyril would have been well aware that in Shenoute he had a forceful and charismatic supporter who loathed and despised Nestorius, and it may also have entered his scheming mind that a Coptic monk who was no great theologian, yet who possessed an iron will and a powerful personality, was no bad companion. What Cyril did not want were objective, unbiased, and learned supporters who appreciated Nestorius' doctrines for what they really were. Had this been so, Cyril's case would have been much weakened, for there is not the least doubt that he deliberately misrepresented Nestorius and did all that he could (which was considerable) to prejudice the case against him. Shenoute was neither objective nor unbiased; his theological competence was questionable; and his knowledge of Nestorianism was confined entirely to popular notions. As far as he was concerned, Nestorius was teaching that Mary gave birth simply to an excellent man, the like of Moses,

David, and others—the heresy commonly known as psilan-
thropism—and was therefore totally denying the incarnation
and all that Christianity stood for.[96] It is understandable that
he would have objected to this, and the fact that Nestorius
never at any time entertained this idea was wholly unknown
to him and therefore wholly irrelevant. As far as Shenoute was
concerned, Nestorius was accursed and should have had his
tongue cut out.[97] He would accept nothing from him, not
even his possessions to give to the poor. 'If you will not
agree with me to confess God', he said, 'I will not agree
with you to take anything from you. You and your possessions are anathema!'[98] Whether Shenoute actually met
Nestorius at Ephesus as Besa describes (see *Vita* 130), and
whether he actually did punch him in the chest remain open
questions (though both events seem most unlikely), but
there is no doubt that the story accurately reflects Shenoute's opinions and character.[99]

In all fairness, however, we must note that Shenoute's
theological inaccuracy was nothing unusual in Upper Egypt.
There was a general and overall lack of knowledge among the
monks of the Thebaid with regard to the problems of the
christological controversy[100], and they could normally be
relied upon to support the Alexandrian patriarch provided
he supported the doctrines which had come out of Nicaea.
Early on in the great controversy, Cyril had persuaded the
Egyptian monks without great difficulty that the title
*Theotokos* or 'God-bearer' as applied to Mary was Nicene
and orthodox, and had also persuaded them that the alleged
refusal of Nestorius to use the term (an allegation which was
quite untrue) implied that Christ was not God.[101] As a consequence of this eminently successful propaganda, he could
rely on the whole-hearted support of the Coptic monks, and
Shenoute stands out at Ephesus not as an isolated individual,
but as the representative of a large and powerful body.

Nestorius was condemned at Ephesus and again at the
great council of Chalcedon twenty years later, but whether

Shenoute was present at the latter council as well as the former is a point of some dispute. Leipoldt, for example, acknowledges that Shenoute was invited to the council by Dioscorus, but maintains that he was mortally ill at the time and, as a consequence, could not have attended.[102] This argument, however, is based in part on Leipoldt's belief that Shenoute died in 451, and if, as we have seen, there is actually good reason to believe that he survived for a further fifteen years, Leipoldt's argument loses much of its force. The view of De Lacy O'Leary that Shenoute did attend the council[103] may be correct. The evidence does not, I think, permit an unequivocal statement either way, but if Shenoute was present, he certainly played no significant role in the synod, and it is quite conceivable that he never really appreciated precisely what was going on.[104]

Shenoute's hatred of heresy in all its forms, real and imaginary, was matched—perhaps exceeded—by his hatred of paganism. Besa tells us more than one tale of his iconoclasm (see *Vita* 83 ff., 125 ff.), and there is not the least doubt that these stories reflect the truth. Upper Egypt was a fairly isolated part of the country. It was culturally less advanced than the Delta, and much that had faded away in the north was still to be found flourishing in the south. Paganism hung on tenaciously in the Thebaid, and especially in the nome of Akhmîm, far longer than in other parts of the country, and Shenoute's obsession with the destruction of polytheism had an abundance of targets on which to be unleashed. His efforts, it seems, were not without success. Although his iconoclastic ferocity brought him once again in confrontation with the local authorities,[105] it was primarily due to Shenoute's attacks, Leipoldt has suggested, that the old gods were no longer revered in Upper Egypt after 451.[106] It is true that their worship had been gradually failing and that their ultimate disappearance was inevitable, but Shenoute seems to have accelerated the process, and he certainly played an important role in establishing Coptic Christianity in all areas and sectors of Upper Egyptian society.

What sort of Christianity did Shenoute teach? We have seen already that he was not an outstanding theologian, and much that was essential to Greek theology and spirituality found no place in his teaching. The idea of *theōsis,* of deification, for example, which is so important in the spirituality of many of the Greek fathers, plays no part in his thinking, and when we examine Shenoute's spiritual teaching the question which comes to mind is not what sort of Christianity it may be, but whether it is Christianity at all. The heart of his teaching is obedience to God. Disobedience is the greatest sin and the mother of all who are dead in sin. Obedience is best seen in humility, cleanliness, truthfulness, peace, obedience to one's superior, and charity; disobedience is manifested in lying, lewdness, theft, violence, idolatry, intoxication, and malice. Obedience is rewarded and brings about God's blessings; disobedience is punished both in this world and in the world to come.[107]

It is understandable, then, that Shenoute laid great stress on the freedom of the human will. We must be free to choose our path if we can truly be said to deserve the consequences of our actions.[108] And it is also understandable why so much of his writing is concerned with making perfectly clear to us what we should do, and equally clear what will happen to us if we do not do it. The choice is ours and ours alone: we may go to heaven or we may go to hell.

What then of Christ's death and the whole concept of mediation and forgiveness? Leipoldt is correct in saying that Shenoute never really appreciated it.[109] True, he quotes the relevant biblical texts about the salvation of sinners and the forgiveness of sins, but these ideas play only a trifling role in his teaching. Christ, for Shenoute, was little more than a suffering figure whose example can provide us with comfort in our own affliction, or a final judge who will come at the end to call us to account.[110] In Besa's *Life,* he is even less: we see him as a magician who can create water where there was no

water (*Vita* 22-23), a convenient source of funds for the
building of a church (*Vita* 30-32), a celestial taxi-driver
who transports Shenoute whithersoever he needs to go
(*Vita* 18, 58), a wonder-worker who raises corpses to satisfy
Shenoute's curiosity (*Vita* 154 ff.), and a revealer of
'mysteries' to his chosen archimandrite (*Vita* 25, 160). It is
this attitude which led Leipoldt to speak of Shenoute's
'christ-less spirituality',[111] and to refer to his christology as a
disaster.[112] Yet it is not something unique to Shenoute, and
was not an uncommon view among the Egyptian ascetics.
Besa's christology is likewise deficient. For him, says Kuhn,
'man faces God and God judges him, indeed is merciful to
him, but the divine actions are unrelated to and unaffected by
the atoning death and resurrection of Christ. The effects of
Christ's work on God, on man, and on the world are ap-
parently ignored'.[113] And in fact, if we look at a great many
of the desert fathers, it is just this Christ-less piety which is
offered to us, and this, in turn, may have something to do
with the curious popularity which these obscure figures are
enjoying at this present time. Shenoute and Besa are in some
ways more Buddhist than Christian: they think in terms of
*karma,* not of mediation. You sow what you reap, and you
work out your own salvation with great care.[114] Do good,
and good will follow you; do ill, and you are doomed.

To assist us in doing good and being obedient to God we
have asceticism and the monastic life, but here we find that
Shenoute's view of these matters is rather more healthy than
that of many of his contemporaries. It is well known that
some of the Egyptian hermits (and more especially those in
Syria) went to absurd and disgusting lengths in practising
their asceticism, and despite the fact that there was general
disapproval of these abnormalities,[115] there is no doubt that
in certain quarters they were very highly regarded. Few
stories are more revolting than that of the brother who, in
tending an old ascetic suffering from a most unpleasant
disease, washed out with water the latter's malodorous sores

and drank the resulting liquid.[116] This is not Shenoute's teaching. Despite his own ascetic predilections, he taught that there was no good in asceticism *per se*.[117] It is the interior attitude, the inner self, which is the key, and more important (and more difficult) than bodily fasting is spiritual fasting, which is control of thoughts. A monk, he says, is a monk by virtue of his good works, not of his habit, and there is little point in trying to reform the church without first reforming the clergy. Reformation is something which begins within and works outwards, not the other way round.[118]

If men were better, in fact, neither fasting nor celibacy would be necessary (after all, the patriarchs married and enjoyed their meals[119]), but since men are not better, and since we have no grounds for assuming that there is going to be any immediate improvement, the cloister and the ascetic life can be a useful means to an end. This is not to say, of course, that life in Shenoute's monastery was an easy option. We have seen already that his rule was stricter than Pjol's, and that Pjol's, in turn, had been stricter than that of Pachomius. For monks living on one meal a day (and that little more than bread and water[120]), fasting was chronic rather than acute, and the incessant labour, recitation, and worship in the White Monastery not only made the cloister self-sufficient, but also trained the monks in obedience (the natural virtue of the *fellahîn*) and kept them out of mischief. The modern Christian's view of asceticism—giving up candies for Lent and cutting down on martinis—is not quite what Shenoute had in mind.

Shenoute's Christianity—if we may call it such—was not unusual for his times or his place. According to Walter Crum, whose knowledge of these matters was long unrivalled, religion in the Thebaid in general involved little more than 'the observance of pious practices and the admiration of ascetic virtues'[121], and the contents of the many Coptic homilies which derive from this and later dates are tediously consistent: uprightness, piety, humility, continence, repentance,

fasting, prayer, and tears.[122] Besa's teaching is the same as Shenoute's: the prevalence and ghastly consequence of sin, exhortations to repent and to live a better life, threats of judgement
and punishment to come, and promises of celestial reward.[123]
There is little more to it than this. 'In Egypt', says A.F. Shore,
'the monastic life failed to mature'[124], and the more one reads
of Shenoute, Besa, and the later ascetics, the more convinced
one becomes of the accuracy of this remark. In the present
writer's view, the Muslim conquest of Egypt in 642 was the
salvation of the country, and the glories of the Caliphate hap-
pily counterbalance the dismal story of Egyptian Christianity
in the fifth and sixth centuries.

Shenoute's death was also the death-knell of the White
Monastery. It survived for a time, partly as a result of the im-
petus given it by Shenoute and partly as a result of the zealous administration of Besa. The contribution of the latter
must not be underrated (he was far more than the archimandrite *bon et simple* of Amélineau[125]), but the fact remains
that he did not have the power and presence of Shenoute,
and his own successor, Zenobius[126], is an obscure figure who
simply accompanies the White Monastery into oblivion. In
Leipoldt's view, the slave-mentality of the uneducated
*fellahîn* could be aroused only by a figure of great force and
charisma, and once that figure had been removed from their
midst, they slowly lapsed back into their customary
apathy.[127] In the fifth century Thebaid, Coptic Christianity
and the name of Shenoute were inseparably linked, and when
he died it was not only Besa and his brethren, but all the
Christians of Upper Egypt, who were left as orphans
(*Vita* 179).

According to Besa, the body of his spiritual father was
shrouded, laid in a chest, and buried (see *Vita* 189; the Arabic
*Life* provides a much more elaborate account), but it was not
to enjoy an undisturbed rest. Precisely what happened to it is
unclear and there is some conflict in the traditions—it may
have been moved when Shīrkūh invaded Egypt in the second
half of the twelfth century, or it may have been translated

to Akhmîm before then[128]—but at some time in the Middle Ages or later it was either lost or destroyed, and all that remains today is the right arm of the saint preserved in the Church of St Shenoute in Old Cairo.[129] Even this fragment is more than we have of Besa, who seems to have disappeared without a trace. Shenoute is commemorated in the Coptic, Ethiopic, and Syriac *Synaxaria,* but elsewhere, as we noted at the beginning of this introduction, his name is unknown and unremembered. Besa's panegyric which is here translated may serve to make the saint a little more familiar, though whether it will make him better appreciated is a different matter. Shenoute is not to everyone's taste and, unlike many of the great lights of Christian spirituality, was very much a product of his times and his place. His appeal to us may be less than his appeal to the *fellahîn,* but whether we like him or not, there can be no doubt that he occupied a very important place in the development of a national and self-conscious Egyptian monasticism.[130] Antony and Pachomius may justly be honoured as the founding fathers of this curious movement, but without Shenoute of Atripe, the archimandrite of the whole world (see *Vita* 9), the picture cannot be complete. We may dislike him, but we can never ignore him. Willingly or unwillingly, we must draw aside the veils of Hellenistic prejudice, and accord this formidable figure due and proper recognition for what he contributed to the development and nature of monastic Christianity in Egypt.

## NOTES

1.  For Shenoute's contribution to Coptic literature, see J. Leipoldt, 'Geschichte der koptischen Literatur' in C. Brockelmann *et al.*, *Geschichte der christlichen Litteraturen des Orients* (Leipzig, 1909) 147-152. Despite its age, this brief account is still useful, but much work still needs to be done in the history of Coptic literature: see especially the important study by T. Orlandi, 'The Future of Studies in Coptic Biblical and Ecclesiastical Literature', in R. McL. Wilson (ed.), *The Future of Coptic Studies* (Leiden, 1978) 143-163.
2.  For editions and translations of Shenoute's works, see the bibliography at the end of this volume.
3.  As J. Leipoldt says in his *Schenute von Atripe und die Entstehung des national ägyptischen Christentums* (Leipzig, 1903) 191, 'Schenute bedeutet für die Weltgeschichte nichts, für die Kopten alles'.
4.  For F. N. Nau's view, see his 'Une version syriaque inédite de la Vie de Schenoudi' in *Revue sémitique d'epigraphie et d'histoire ancienne* 7 (1899) 356-363, and for its refutation see Leipoldt, *Schenute* 16 and the same author's edition of the Bohairic text of Besa's *Life* (J. Leipoldt and W. E. Crum, eds., *Sinuthii Archimandritae Vita et Opera Omnia I* [CSCO 41/Copt. 1; Paris, 1906]) 2. See also P. Ladeuze, *Étude sur le cénobitisme Pakhomien pendant le IVe siècle et la première moitié du Ve* (Louvain, 1898; rpt. Frankfurt am Main, 1961) 122-124.
5.  For Besa, his work, his teaching, and his importance, see K. H. Kuhn, 'A Fifth-Century Egyptian Abbot' in *Journal of Theological Studies,* NS 5 (1954) 36-48 (=pt. 1), 174-187 (=pt. 2); 6 (1955) 35-48 (=pt. 3). The whole of this tripartite study is devoted to Besa and it supercedes all earlier work (e.g. P. van Cauwenbergh, *Étude sur les moines d'Égypte depuis le concile de Chalcédoine (451) jusqu'à l'invasion arabe (640)* [Paris, 1914; rpt. Milan, 1973] 2-6, 137-151). Kuhn has also translated all that remains of Besa's own writing: see K. H. Kuhn, *Letters and*

24

*Sermons of Besa* (CSCO 157; Louvain, 1956 [Coptic text];
CSCO 158; Louvain, 1956 [English translation]).

6. These references refer to the Notes to the translation.
7. These references refer to the section numbers of the translation itself.
8. For a description of the White Monastery, see Leipoldt, *Schenute* 92-99; A. J. Butler, *The Ancient Coptic Churches of Egypt* (Oxford, 1884; rpt. 1970) 1:351-359; O. F. A. Meinardus, *Christian Egypt: Ancient and Modern* (Cairo, 1977²) 401-404; and C. C. Walters, *Monastic Archaeology in Egypt* (Warminster, 1974) Index s.v. 'Deir el Abiad'. For further bibliographical information, see Walters, 241. Both Meinardus and Walters provide numerous photographs, and four other illustrations may be found in J. G. Milne, *A History of Egypt Under Roman Rule* (London, 1924³) 106, 224, 225, 226.
9. E. Amélineau, *Les moines égyptiens: Vie de Schnoudi* (Paris, 1889) 83.
10. See nn. 46-47 below.
11. See Dioscorus' encomium on Macarius of Tkoou in E. Amélineau, *Monuments pour servir à l'histoire de l'Égypte chrétienne aux IVᵉ, Vᵉ, VIᵉ et VIIᵉ siècles (Mémoires de la mission archéologique française au Caire* 4 [Paris, 1888-1894]) 1:110. It seems that during Shenoute's lifetime, Besa had already attained a position of trust and responsibility (see Kuhn, 'Fifth-Century Egyptian Abbot' pt. 1:39).
12. See n. 39 below.
13. See n. 5 above.
14. See Kuhn, 'Fifth-Century Egyptian Abbot' pt. 1:38; van Cauwenbergh, *Étude sur les moines* 138-139.
15. See Kuhn, 'Fifth-Century Egyptian Abbot' pt. 1:39.
16. See *ibid.* pt. 1:39 n. 6.
17. See Ladeuze, *Étude sur le cénobitisme* 117. The fragments are collected and translated in Amélineau's *Monuments.* It was the opinion of the latter that one of these fragments indicated the existence of a second Sahidic *Life* quite different from that of Besa (see *Monuments* 1:247), but Ladeuze has demonstrated that this is not necessarily so (Ladeuze, 125 n. 1). The fragment from the *Life of Pijimi* translated in the notes to the translation n. 91, for example, could easily be mistaken for part of another *Vita* of Shenoute if we had no idea of its context and provenance. On the other hand, since Shenoute was a well-known figure, it is certainly not impossible that there should have been other

*Lives;* but as yet we lack incontrovertible evidence.

18. See Leipoldt and Crum's edition of the Bohairic text of Besa's *Life* (see n. 4 above) 2-3.

19. See Amélineau, *Monuments* 1:1-91.

20. See n. 4 above.

21. For the text and translation of the Arabic *Life,* see Amélineau, *Monuments* 1:289-478. This is not a particularly satisfactory edition. There are other manuscripts of this *Life* which differ not only from Amélineau's text, but also among themselves. But for the present, Amélineau's version is the only one we have in print.

22. See *ibid.* 1: vii ff., and the same author's *Vie de Schnoudi* 230.

23. See Leipoldt, *Schenute* 14, and Ladeuze, *Étude sur le cénobitisme* 124-127.

24. See Leipoldt, *Schenute* 14-15; Ladeuze, *Étude sur le cénobitisme* 127-136; Nau, 'Une version syriaque . . .' 348-361.

25. See Amélineau, *Vie de Schnoudi* 185-187; he refers there to the episode somewhat romantically as 'the most beautiful page of [Shenoute's] life' (187).

26. This has been stressed by Leipoldt, *Schenute* 14 and Ladeuze, *Étude sur le cénobitisme* 141-143.

27. See Amélineau, *Monuments* 1:331.

28. See Leipoldt, *Schenute* 93-94, but it is only fair to point out that in Ladeuze' view, they have been exaggerated (see Ladeuze, *Étude sur le cénobitisme* 209). For a very sound account of the large numbers of monks in early Christian Egypt, see H. Bacht, 'Die Rolle des orientalischen Mönchtums in den kirchen-politischen Auseinandersetzungen um Chalkedon (431-519)' in A. Grillmeier and H. Bacht (eds.), *Das Konzil von Chalkedon: Geschichte und Gegenwart* (Würzburg, 1954) 2:292-296. In 1971, the total number had shrunk to about 350 (see Meinardus, *Christian Egypt: Ancient and Modern* 15).

29. See Amélineau, *Vie de Schnoudi* xiv-xv. On page x, he compares this form of literature to *chansons de geste.*

30. This was published in the *Gesellschaft der Wissenschaften zu Göttingen. Nachrichten* 3 (1889) 49-56.

31. See his 'Une version syriaque . . . ' in *Revue sémitique . . .* 7 (1899) 356-363; 8 (1900) 153-167, 252-265.

32. For a brief discussion of the Syriac *Lives,* see Leipoldt, *Schenute* 15-16 as well as the articles by Guidi and Nau cited in nn. 30 and 31 above.

33. The earlier version was entitled *Schenute, der Begründer der national ägyptischen Kirche* (Leipzig, 1903); for the title of the

later version, which is more than twice as long as the earlier, see n. 3 above. All references in these notes are to the later edition.

34. There are two other early studies of some length which are worthy of mention: (i) the material in Ladeuze, *Étude sur le cénobitisme* 116-154, 206-221, 241-254, 305-326, 348-357; and (ii) the lengthy article by Eugène Revillout, 'Les origines du schisme égyptien, premier récit: le précurseur et inspirateur Sénuti le prophète', in *Revue de l'histoire des religions* 8 (1883) 401-467, 545-581. These studies, especially that of Ladeuze, are still of considerable use, but they must be treated with much greater caution than Leipoldt's work.

35. *Shenoute* (Sahidic)/*Shenouti* (Bohairic) = *She* + *noute/nouti*. *She* is a shortened form of *shēre/shēri* (= Egyptian šri) 'son', and *noute/nouti* (= Egyptian *ntr*) means 'god'.

36. See Ladeuze, *Étude sur le cénobitisme* 241-251: 'L'archimandrite d'Atripé mourut donc peu de temps après le concile de Chalcédoine, le 1er juillet 452' (251).

37. See Leipoldt, *Schenute* 44-47. This is also the date suggested by Amélineau.

38. See Nau, 'Une version Syriaque . . . ' 356 n. 1.

39. See J. F. Bethune-Baker, 'The Date of the Death of Nestorius: Schenute, Zacharias, Evagrius' in *Journal of Theological Studies* OS 9 (1908) 601-605.

40. It seems at first glance that there is a disagreement between Besa's statement and that in the Arabic *Life* which gives the age of Shenoute at his death as 109 years and 2 months (see Amélineau, *Monuments* 1:467). There may actually be no disagreement at all, for it is probable that the Arabic *Life* is counting the years not from Shenoute's birth, but from his entry into the White Monastery which, as we shall see a little later (see note 48 below), was said to have occurred when he was nine. Some confirmation for this view is to be found in Dioscorus' encomium on Macarius of Tkoou which says specifically that Shenoute died in the 109th year after his profession (see Amélineau, *Monuments* 1:110-111 and Ladeuze, *Étude sur le cénobitisme* 241-244).

41. There is an inscription in the White Monastery which gives the date of Shenoute's birth as the sixty-fifth year of the era of the martyrs, and this corresponds to 349 CE (see W. E. Crum, 'Inscriptions from Shenoute's Monastery' in *Journal of Theological Studies* OS 5 [1904] 555-556). But Crum was doubtful whether this date could be accepted since it could not be reconciled with Leipoldt's calculations (see *ibid.* 556). Crum's

article, however, was published before that of Bethune-Baker
which, as we have seen, offered a revised date for Shenoute's
death (see n. 39 above), and if we accept the latter's arguments,
it may well be that this inscription represents an authentic
tradition.

42. See Leipoldt, *Schenute* 43, 46-47.

43. See *The Lives of the Desert Fathers: The Historia Monachorum in
Aegypto*, tr. N. Russell (CS 34; Kalamazoo/Oxford, 1981) 54
(= I, 17).

44. According to Palladius, John retired from the world at about
twenty-five, withdrew to his mountain cell at Lycopolis some five
years later, and shortly before his death told Palladius that he had
been in that cell for forty years 'never beholding a woman's face
or the sight of money' (*Palladius: The Lausiac History*, tr. R. T.
Meyer [Westminster, 1965] 99, 102-103 [= XXXV, 1 and 13]).

45. For the Coptic fragment, see D. W. Johnson, 'Further Fragments
of a Coptic History of the Church: Cambridge OR. 1699R' in
*Enchoria* 6 (1976) 9 (text), 15 (translation): '[Apa Shenoute]
himself sat in the synod which had taken place in the city of
Ephesus . . . ' . This passage is not to be found in the collection of
the fragments of this history compiled, edited, and translated by
Tito Orlandi in the two volumes of his *Storia della chiesa di
Alessandria (Testi e documenti per lo studio dell'antichità
XVII, XXXI; Milan, 1968, 1970*). In fact, the name of Shenoute
occurs nowhere in this collection. For the text and translation of
Severus' *History of the Patriarchs* pertaining to this period, see
B. Evetts (ed./tr.), *History of the Patriarchs of the Coptic Church
of Alexandria, II: Peter I to Benjamin I (661) (Patrologia
Orientalis* I/4; Paris, 1948) Again, there is no mention of
Shenoute.

46. See Leipoldt, *Schenute* 42-44.

47. See *ibid.* 43-44, and De Lacy O'Leary, *The Saints of Egypt*
(London, 1937; rpt. Amsterdam, 1974) 252. This is also the
view of Meinardus: see his *Christian Egypt: Ancient and Modern*
402.

48. See Amélineau, *Monuments* 1:468; Leipoldt, *Schenute* 40 n. 5.
One of the inscriptions in the White Monastery also follows this
tradition (see Crum, 'Inscriptions . . . ' 554-555).

49. Leipoldt suggests that Shenoute's parents died early in his life
(*Schenute* 40), and Amélineau that they were old when he was
born (*Vie de Schnoudi* 15).

50. Leipoldt, for example, considers it most unlikely that Shenoute

retired to the inner desert for an unbroken period of five years (see his *Schenute* 104 n. 5).

51. For Amélineau's view, see his *Vie de Schnoudi* 80, but, as Leipoldt says, in reading this *Vie* we must marvel not at Amélineau's knowledge of his sources, but at his imagination! (*Schenute* 21). Ladeuze has a similar view: 'We know absolutely nothing', he says, 'of the first years [Shenoute] passed in the monastic life', but he adds that this did not prevent Amélineau from devoting thirty pages to the matter in his *Vie de Schnoudi* (see Ledeuze, *Étude sur le cénobitisme* 207). The question of the nature and existence of a novitiate in Egyptian monasteries of the period is a difficult one and it would be out of place to examine it in detail here. There is a useful discussion in Leipoldt, *Schenute* 106-113, and it seems more than likely that Shenoute himself had much to do with the establishment and organization of this institution.

52. Leipoldt, *Schenute* 1.

53. Amélineau, *Vie de Schnoudi* 62.

54. *Ibid.* 58.

55. See Leipoldt, *Schenute* 47-53, and the same author's comments in Brockelmann *et al., Geschichte der christlichen Litteraturen des Orients* 148.

56. See Leipoldt, *Schenute* 102: 'Seine pedantische Gewissenhaftigkeit . . .'.

57. For the Coptic text, see *ibid.* 195-196 or CSCO 42 (Copt. 2) [1908] 20, and for a slightly different English translation, see Kuhn, 'Fifth-Century Egyptian Abbot' pt. 2: 175. The covenant demanded by Besa was a little shorter: 'We will not steal, we will not lie, we will not defile our body in any way, we will not bear false witness, we will not do anything deceitful secretly, and all the other words which come after these' (*ibid.*) For a discussion of Shenoute's covenant, see Leipoldt, *Schenute* 108-110.

58. See *ibid.* 141-143 for a translation and discussion of this letter.

59. See *ibid.* 143; Ladeuze, *Étude sur le cénobitisme* 218; Amélineau, *Vie de Schnoudi* 279. The monk concerned was guilty of no more than a minor theft and a trivial lie.

60. On opposition to Shenoute and disturbances at the White Monastery, see Leipoldt, *Schenute* 50-52, 149-155; Ladeuze, *Étude sur le cénobitisme* 215-216; Amélineau, *Vie de Schnoudi* 131-148, 274-275; for similar opposition to Besa, see Kuhn, 'Fifth-Century Egyptian Abbot' pt. 2: 180, 181, 183.

61. See Leipoldt, *Schenute* 150.

62. See, for example, Kuhn, 'Fifth-Century Egyptian Abbot' pt. 2: 174, 175.

63. See Leipoldt, *Schenute* 65, 186-188.

64. This is Amélineau's comment: see his *Vie de Schnoudi* 303.

65. O'Leary, *Saints of Egypt* 252.

66. See Leipoldt, *Schenute* 190. Cf. Kuhn, 'Fifth-Century Egyptian Abbot' pt. 3:48: 'By continuing Shenoute's policy of teaching the monks and nuns to read and understand the Scriptures, Besa made his monastery an oasis of learning in the midst of the ignorance of the peasantry amongst whom it was situated'. The ability to read was one of the most important things—sometimes the only thing—which distinguished the monk from the *fellah* (see Leipoldt, *Schenute* 43 n. 1).

67. For an excellent discussion of these various trades and occupations, see H. E. Winlock and W. E. Crum, *The Monastery of Epiphanius at Thebes* (New York, 1926; rpt. 1973) 1:51-97, 155-166. See also Walters, *Monastic Archaeology* 219-223; W. H. C. Frend, *The Rise of the Monophysite Movement* (Cambridge, 1972) 80; and Kuhn, 'Fifth-Century Egyptian Abbot' pt. 2:185 (dealing with trades at the White Monastery under Besa).

68. This is Leipoldt's estimate (= about 50 sq. km.): see *Schenute* 95-96 for his ingenious argument. Kuhn also accepts this figure ('Fifth-Century Egyptian Abbot' pt. 1:37).

69. See Leipoldt, *Schenute* 174-175, 191. Further on the economic importance of the monasteries in Egypt, see A. H. M. Jones, *The Later Roman Empire 284-602* (Oxford, 1964) 2:931-932, and Kuhn, 'Fifth-Century Egyptian Abbot' pt. 2:185.

70. On the frequency of theft at the White Monastery under Shenoute and Besa, see Leipoldt, *Schenute* 144, 150, and Kuhn, 'Fifth-Century Egyptian Abbot' pt. 2:178.

71. See Leipoldt, *Schenute* 150-151 for examples and discussion of this opposition.

72. See Amélineau, *Vie de Schnoudi* 275.

73. See Leipoldt, *Schenute* 1-2.

74. See *ibid.* 152-153.

75. See, for example, the studies by D. W. Young, A. Shisha-Halevy, E. Lucchesi, and H. Quecke listed in the bibliography at the end of this volume.

76. For descriptions of Shenoute's style, see A. Shisha-Halevy, 'Unpublished Shenoutiana in the British Library' in *Enchoria* 5 (1975) 96 n. 23, and Leipoldt, *Schenute* 58-62.

77. See W. E. Crum. 'A Study in the History of Egyptian Monas-

ticism' in *Journal of Theological Studies* OS 5 (1904) 133. This article is a review of Leipoldt's *Schenute*.

78. See Winlock/Crum, *Monastery of Epiphanius* 1:166.
79. See *ibid.* 167. It appears to have been a standard requirement that a deacon should learn at least one gospel by heart, and it would seem that it took about two months to memorize the gospel of John (see W. E. Crum, *Coptic Ostraca from the Collections of the Egypt Exploration Fund, the Cairo Museum and Others* [London, 1902] #30, #31 [for the gospel of Matthew], #Ad. 7 [for the gospel of Mark]). Aphou of Oxyrhynchus was more severe: his deacons had to learn twenty-five psalms and two Pauline epistles, as well as a section of John's gospel (see *ibid.* 9 n. 5).
80. For a sound discussion of bilingualism in Egypt, see Jones, *Later Roman Empire* 2:994-996. See also the useful materials pertaining to the Thebaid in Winlock/Crum, *Monastery of Epiphanius* 1:143, 196.
81. See Leipoldt, *Schenute* 94-95.
82. See *ibid.* 71; the same author's introduction to the Bohairic text of Besa's *Life* (see n. 4 above) 2; Amélineau, *Vie de Schnoudi* 50-51.
83. For a discussion, see Kuhn, 'Fifth-Century Egyptian Abbot' pt. 1:45.
84. See Leipoldt, *Schenute* 72. But Shenoute can and does use Platonic argumentation and considerable skill and effect: see the lengthy discussion in E. Amélineau, *Oeuvres de Shenoudi* (Paris, 1907-14) 2:329-460.
85. See A. Erman, 'Schenute und Aristophanes' in *Zeitschrift für aegyptische Sprache* 32 (1894) 134-135.
86. See U. Treu, 'Aristophanes bei Schenute' in *Philologus: Zeitschrift für das klassische Altertum* 101 (1957) 325-328.
87. See A. van Lantschoot, 'A propos du *Physiologus*' in *Coptic Studies in Honor of Walter Ewing Crum* (Boston, 1950) 339-363, especially 363, and P. du Bourguet, 'Diatribe de Chenouté contre le démon' in *Société d'archéologie copte. Bulletin* 16 (1961-62) 21.
88. See van Lantschoot, 'A propos du *Physiologus*' *passim,* and the same author's 'Fragments syriaques du *Physiologus*' in *Muséon* 72 (1959) 37-52.
89. For Athanasius, see Leipoldt, *Schenute* 86, and L. T. Lefort, 'Athanase, Ambroise, et Chenouté: "Sur la virginité" ' in *Muséon* 48 (1935) 55-74; for the letters of Antony, see G. Ga-

ritte, 'A propos des lettres de saint Antoine l'ermite' in *Muséon* 52 (1939) 11-31; for the letters of Pachomius, see Leipoldt, *Schenute* 86 n. 4; for Evagrius, see du Bourguet, 'Diatribe' 21.

90. For Origen, see Leipoldt, *Schenute* 86 (and see also H. Thompson, 'Dioscorus and Shenoute' in *École pratique des hautes études. Bibliothèque* 234 [1922] 374-376), and du Bourguet, 'Diatribe' 48; for the *Acts of Archelaus* and the *Gospel of Thomas*, see D. W. Young, 'The Milieu of Nag Hammadi: Some Historical Considerations' in *Vigilae Christianae* 24 (1970) 127-137.

91. See L. T. Lefort, 'Catéchèse Christologique de Chenouté' in *Zeitschrift für aegyptische Sprache* 80 (1955) 40-55.

92. See du Bourguet, 'Diatribe' 21-22: 'Chenouté s'y révèle, une fois de plus [and du Bourguet here cites Lefort's article], théologien averti et souvent original . . . ' . We may compare the comment of O. F. A. Meinardus in his *Christian Egypt: Faith and Life* (Cairo, 1970) 198 that Shenoute was 'a theologian of distinction and originality'. He might not have been as bad as Leipoldt paints him, but such comments as these are surely going too far.

93. Shenoute is quoting Proverbs 30:18-19. See Leipoldt, *Schenute* 73 for a translation of the text.

94. See *ibid.*

95. See *ibid.* 90.

96. See *ibid.* 88 and Lefort, 'Catéchèse christologique' 43 [text], 45 [translation]: 'Nestorius himself, to whom has been given the name of bishop, and others of his sort . . . have said that [Mary] brought forth a good (*chrēstos*) man, the like of Moses and David and others'. As I have indicated, there is a play on words here: the term for 'good' *chrēstos* (a Greek loan-word), differs by only a single letter from the title of Christ, *Christos*.

97. See Bethune-Baker, 'Date of the Death of Nestorius' 604, for an English translation of the relevant passage which occurs in Dioscorus' encomium on Macarius of Tkoou. Shenoute's comment may have given rise to some peculiar ideas as to how Nestorius died (*ibid.* 603).

98. This is translated from the fragments of the Coptic history of the church cited in n. 45 above (Johnson, 'Further Fragments' 9 [text], 15 [translation]). The same dialogue is to be found in the encomium on Macarius of Tkoou (see Bethune-Baker, 'Date of the Death of Nestorius', 604), whence the author of the Coptic history probably borrowed it.

99. So far as we know at present, Cyril and Nestorius never met at any session of the council of Ephesus, and if Shenoute was with Cyril, he is not likely to have met Nestorius either. Leipoldt considers the story wholly fictitious (*Schenute* 1 n. 2), as does Ladeuze (*Étude sur le cénobitisme* 140), and Revillout ('Origines du schisme égyptien' 550).

100. See Winlock/Crum, *Monastery of Epiphanius* 1:153; Kuhn, 'Fifth-Century Egyptian Abbot' pt. 3:35; van Cauwenbergh, *Étude sur les moines* 171.

101. See Frend, *Rise of the Monophysite Movement* 139.

102. See Leipoldt, *Schenute* 42, 90. This view is accepted by Heinrich Bacht in his 'Die Rolle des orientalischen Mönchtums' 236.

103. See O'Leary, *Saints of Egypt* 253.

104. According to the Arabic *Life,* Shenoute was invited to Chalcedon, but was ill in bed at the time. He then received a visit from Christ who came down from heaven to talk with him and comfort him (no uncommon occurrence for our hero). Shenoute, therefore, asked Christ to give him the strength to go to the council as he had been summoned by the patriarch (Dioscorus) to expose the errors which were being taught by heretics like Arius with regard to the Trinity, but Christ explained that he had other plans for him, namely, his demise and his return to the celestial homeland (see Amélineau, *Monuments* 1:467-468). The point of this story (which appears, once again, to derive from the encomium on Macarius of Tkoou) is not its questionable historical veracity, but what it reveals of the writer's knowledge of the council of Chalcedon. This council was little concerned with the matter of the Trinity, and Athanasius and the Cappadocian Fathers had long since put paid to the subordinationism of Arius.

105. Amélineau tells the tale (based on the Arabic *Life*) in his *Vie de Schnoudi* 317-319.

106. See Leipoldt, *Schenute* 182.

107. See generally *ibid.* 74-77. Leipoldt provides translations of the relevant passages.

108. See *ibid.* 78-79. This is also true of Besa: see Kuhn, 'Fifth-Century Egyptian Abbot' pt. 3:41-42. It follows from this that sins committed in ignorance are not punished; we must know what we are doing (see du Bourguet, 'Diatribe' 36 [text], 47 [translation]).

109. See Leipoldt, *Schenute* 80-81.

110. See *ibid.* 81.

111. *Ibid.* 82: 'seine sozusagen christuslose Frömmigkeit'.
112. See *ibid.* Similarly, in *ibid.* 81, he speaks of Shenoute's 'desolate Christology' (*öden Christologie*).
113. Kuhn, 'Fifth-Century Egyptian Abbot' pt. 3:46.
114. Cf. the Buddha's last words as reported in *Dīgha Nikāya* ii 154. They do not appear in the Sarvāstivāda Sanskrit version, and the Chinese translations are in some cases rather more elaborate.
115. See D. J. Chitty, *The Desert a City* (Oxford, 1966; rpt. 1977) 30, 44 n. 150.
116. See M. Chaîne, *Le manuscrit de la version copte en dialecte Sahidique des Apophthegmata Patrum* (Cairo, 1960) 38 #171 (text), 116-117 #171 (translation).
117. See Leipoldt, *Schenute* 66, and *ibid.* 62-69 generally. Shenoute, we might add, was not the only one of these early fathers who failed to practise what he preached, and there is no doubt that the idea that extreme asceticism was not something good in itself ran counter to prevailing and popular opinion. As Leipoldt says, Shenoute's own regimen seems to invalidate his teaching, 'but who could withstand the spirit of the times?' (*ibid.* 69).
118. For translations of the relevant passages, see *ibid.* 66-67, 184-186. Leipoldt was, of course, aware that these ideas were not confined to Shenoute. The point he makes is that whereas for others (such as Theodore or Horsiesios) these views were important, for Shenoute they were fundamental (see *ibid.* 66 n. 2).
119. See *ibid.* 67-68.
120. For an excellent and detailed account of the dietary and fasting practices of monks in the Thebaid, see Winlock/Crum, *Monastery of Epiphanius* 1:144-149, 170-171. Crum calls bread and salt 'the proverbial diet of Theban ascetes' (*ibid.* 170). For a more specific discussion of practices at the White Monastery, see Leipoldt, *Schenute* 116-120.
121. Winlock/Crum, *Monastery of Epiphanius* 1:153.
122. See W. R. Dawson, 'Early Christianity in Egypt: The Literature of the Coptic Period' in *The Asiatic Review* NS 17 (1921) 345, summarizing the contents of the homilies edited and translated (not very satisfactorily) by Wallis Budge in 1910 (E. A. Wallis Budge, *Coptic Homilies in the Dialect of Upper Egypt* [London, 1910]).
123. See Kuhn, 'Fifth-Century Egyptian Abbot' pt. 1:42, pt. 3:44-45.
124. A. F. Shore, 'Christian and Coptic Egypt' in J. R. Harris (ed.), *The Legacy of Egypt* (Oxford, 1971²) 409.
125. See Amélineau, *Vie de Schnoudi* 229.

126. See Crum, 'Study in the History of Egyptian Monasticism' 132; van Cauwenbergh, *Étude sur les moines* 139; Kuhn, 'Fifth-Century Egyptian Abbot' pt. 1:38.
127. See Leipoldt, *Schenute* 190.
128. See Meinardus, *Christian Egypt: Faith and Life* 148, 189.
129. See *ibid.* 189.
130. Cf. Frend, *Rise of the Monophysite Movement* 72-73: 'With [Shenoute] one can detect the growth of a self-conscious Coptic spirit growing away even linguistically from the previously dominant Greek, and which combined Monophysitism and prophecy as formidable weapons against outsiders. Shenoute's work, too, of gathering in the traditional riff-raff of Egyptian society and giving its members the standing of monks and an assurance of personal salvation, as well as his passionate eloquence in their native tongue, provided the Monophysite movement in Egypt with a popular basis that it never lost'.

## A NOTE ON THE TRANSLATION

The language of the Bohairic version of Besa's *Life of Shenoute* is fairly straightforward, and apart from a few curious words and an occasional odd construction, offers no real difficulties to a translator. I would point out, however, that this present English version is not intended for the linguist, but for a more general audience, and I have therefore translated certain passages a little more freely than I might otherwise have done. The Coptic conjugation system is capable of considerable subtlety (see, for example, the excellent survey by H. J. Polotsky, 'The Coptic Conjugation System' in *Orientalia* 29 [1960] 392-422), but to bring out this subtlety in English frequently demands cumbersome constructions which, in the present circumstances, are better avoided. It is also true that whereas Coptic prose has a certain distinct style and rhythm, it is not a style or rhythm which can readily be appreciated in English. I have had no hesitation, therefore, in breaking up the sometimes overlong Coptic sentences into more readily digestible sections. Nor have I thought it necessary to reproduce every Greek *de* and Coptic *on*. It is actually much easier to produce a 'crib' than a translation, but a crib makes tiresome reading, and Besa deserves more than that. If I have failed to do him justice, the fault is mine, not his.

DNB

1982

# TRANSCRIPTION OF GREEK AND COPTIC

| | |
|---|---|
| alpha | a |
| beta | b |
| gamma | g |
| delta | d |
| epsilon | e |
| zeta | z |
| ēta | ē |
| theta | th |
| iota | i |
| kappa | k |
| lambda | l |
| mu | m |
| nu | n |
| xi | x |
| omicron | o |
| pi | p |
| rho | r |
| sigma | s |
| tau | t |
| upsilon | u |
| phi | ph |
| chi | ch |
| psi | ps |
| ōmega | ō |

---

| | |
|---|---|
| shai | š |
| fai | f |
| khai | kh |
| hori | h |
| jenja | j |
| ǧima | ǧ |
| ti | ti |

BESA

THE LIFE OF SHENOUTE

**1.** A FEW OF THE MIRACLES AND MARVELS
WHICH GOD EFFECTED THROUGH OUR HOLY
FATHER THE PROPHET[1] APA[2] SHENOUTE,
THE PRIEST AND ARCHIMANDRITE, WHICH
THE HOLY APA BESA, HIS DISCIPLE, RE-
LATED TO THE GLORY OF GOD AND THE
PROFIT OF ALL WHO WILL HEAR THEM, SO
THAT THEY MAY GLORIFY GOD AT ALL
TIMES, BUT ESPECIALLY ON THE DAY OF
HIS HOLY COMMEMORATION, THE SEVENTH
DAY OF THE MONTH EPIPHI.[3] IN THE PEACE
OF GOD. AMEN.

**2.** I will begin my account of the miracles and marvels which God effected through our blessed and holy father apa Shenoute, those which I, Besa, his disciple, saw with my own eyes and also the others which our holy father apa Shenoute told me with his own mouth, in which there is no guile.* It is these from which I will now offer you a small selection. Come, and we will reveal to you now the miracles and marvels which God worked through my father the old man.[4] Behold, I am burdened and troubled with many years, and since I am feeble and unskilled in speaking, I am afraid to go into the wondrous works of my father apa Shenoute, lest I be plunged into the waters of the sea[5] without knowing how to swim. Although I owe a great debt, the creditor is not concerned for his things, for my father apa Shenoute of good memory, whose [feast] we celebrate today, is worthy to have his good works related, and also his asceticism, his

---

*Cf. Rv 14:5

way of life,[6] his admirable virtues, and the great and incredible signs, just like those of the holy prophets and the apostles of the Lord, which he brought about.

**3.** There was a village called Šenalolet[7] in the nome[8] of Šmin,[9] and there lived the righteous parents of our blessed father. The father of apa Shenoute was a farmer who had a few sheep, and he gave them to a shepherd to look after them in the field. Now the shepherd said to the father of apa Shenoute: 'Give me your boy Shenoute to watch over the sheep with me, and I will give you a little of my wages for him'. The young boy Shenoute had then begun to grow up in the grace of God which was in him and was gradually becoming more and more attractive. The mother of the young boy Shenoute said to the shepherd: 'Look, I will give my son to you, but send him back to me at the evening of each day. He is my only son, and I rejoice to God with him night and day'. And the shepherd said to them: 'Every day, before the sun sets, I will send him back to you'. So henceforth, the shepherd took the boy Shenoute and looked after the sheep with him, and each day, when evening came, the shepherd would send the boy Shenoute back to his parents in the village.

**4.** Now apa Shenoute himself used to go down into a water-cistern a short distance from the village—it was during the month of Tybi[10]—stretch out his hands and pray like that, with the water coming up to his neck. Every day, therefore, when it was getting light, the mother and father of the young boy would quarrel with the shepherd, saying: 'Why did you not send our son back to us at evening? We were afraid that something evil had happened to him'. Then the shepherd would say to his parents: 'Truly, I do send him back to you every evening'. On one of these days, then, the shepherd followed the young boy Shenoute until he arrived at the water-cistern, and by the water-cistern there was a sycamore tree. Then the boy went down into the water and there prayed to God with his hands stretched up to heaven. The shepherd followed him and hid himself under the sycamore tree so as to see what the young boy was doing. The shepherd would [often] testify and say: 'I saw the young boy's ten fingers like ten flaming lamps, so I returned and went back beside my sheep. In the morning (he said) his father came and again quarrelled with me, saying: "Why did you not send my son back to me at evening?" I said to him: "Take your son with you! I am not worthy to have him stay with me! And his father took him home".' This is what the shepherd told us when he testified to us.

**5.** Ten days after these things had occurred, his father took him to the holy apa Pjol[11] to receive his blessing. When they still had a mile to go on the road which led to the place of apa Pjol, [the latter was there] teaching what was good for the soul to a large group of the rulers of Smin whom he had agreed to meet there.[12] The holy apa Pjol said to the men sitting by him: 'Arise, let us go out to the archimandrite'. So the holy apa Pjol and the men sitting by him got up and went outside, and when apa Pjol came to apa Shenoute, he took apa Shenoute's hand and placed it on his head, saying: 'Bless me, my father and archimandrite!' And they went inside and sat down.

**6.** At that time there was a man sitting by apa Pjol who had within him an unclean spirit, and when the young boy saw the spirit which was in the man, he stretched out his hand, seized a small sounding-board,[13] and began to beat the demon which was in the man. The evil spirit cried out, saying: 'I will flee from your face, O Shenoute, for truly, from the time I saw you, fire has devoured me!' And at that very moment the spirit departed from the man, and he regained his health and gave glory to the good God. Apa Pjol said to the young boy Shenoute: 'Wait until the time comes, my son'.

**7.** After these events, apa Pjol spoke with the apa Shenoute's father and said: 'Let the young boy stay with me this week, and [then] come for him', and because apa Shenoute's mother was apa Pjol's sister, born of the [same] father and mother, he left [Shenoute] with him.

**8.** At evening on that day, apa Pjol lay down alone in a certain place, and he also gave the young boy Shenoute a place [to lie down] alone. But when apa Pjol raised his eyes to heaven, he saw an angel of the Lord guarding the young boy Shenoute while he was sleeping, and the angel said to apa Pjol: 'When you get up in the morning, put the mantle which you will find before you upon the young boy Shenoute, for it is the mantle of Elijah the Tishbite which the Lord Jesus has sent to you to put upon him. Truly, he will be a righteous and illustrious man, and after him, no-one like him will arise in any country. He will build a monastery, and to everyone who enters his place will he be a comfort and a protection; his community will endure for [all] generations.' When apa Pjol arose in the morning, he took the mantle which he found before him, called apa Shenoute and put it upon him; and having made him a monk, he kept him with him.

**9.** A few days after this, when they were dwelling together, the holy apa Pjol and the young man Shenoute went out walking together, and with them also went apa Pšoi from Mt Psōou.[14] He too was a holy man who walked after godly things. When these three—apa Pjol and apa Shenoute and apa Pšoi—were walking together, there came to them a voice from heaven saying: 'Today Shenoute was appointed archimandrite of the whole world'. Apa Pjol said to apa Pšoi: 'My brother Pšoi, did you too hear this voice which just now came from heaven?' Apa Pšoi said to apa Pjol: 'Indeed I did'. And when they had agreed between them as to what they had heard, apa Pjol said to apa Pšoi: 'Let us ask the young boy Shenoute as well'. And they asked him: 'Did you hear this voice which just now came from heaven?' 'Indeed I did', he said. Apa Pjol said to him: 'What was it you heard?' Apa Shenoute, without the least guile, said to apa Pjol: 'I heard, "Today Shenoute was appointed archimandrite of the whole world"'. Apa Pjol and apa Pšoi were greatly astonished and glorified God, saying: 'Truly, he will be wholly perfect!'

**10.** When the holy apa Shenoute had received the angelic garment which came to him from heaven, he gave himself up to the anchoretic life with many great labours, many nocturnal vigils, and fasts without number. Nor would he eat each day until the sun had set at evening, and then he would not eat his fill; instead, his food was bread and salt. Because of these things, his body was dried up, and his skin was very fine and stuck to his bones. The whole of his life and his intention were like [those of] Elijah the Tishbite, the charioteer of Israel.*

**11.** In this way, as he was always so zealous in his labours, he was a teacher of all, not only of the young boys, but also of the old men. He bore Christ, persevering in the recitation of the Scriptures and, as a consequence, his renown and his teachings were sweet in everyone's mouth, like honey to the heart of those who seek to love eternal life. He would deliver[15] many expositions and discourses full of holy precepts; he established rules for the monks and [wrote] salty letters,† and brought both fear and comfort to the souls of men. And of everything which came from his mouth (in which there was no guile),** he said: 'No word that I utter comes from myself alone; there is none which Christ does not deliver to me'.

**12.** He adorned his life gloriously with the perfection of monastic labours, great asceticism, and a multitude of [ascetic] practices,[16] for he would pray twelve times a day, making twenty-four prostrations each time. At night he would not sleep at all until day-break; afterwards, for the sake of his body, he would sleep just a little so that it would not perish [too] quickly. There were many times when he did not eat from Saturday to Saturday, and again, for the forty

---

*Cf. 2 K 2:12
† Cf. Col 4:6
** Cf. Rv 14:5

days of holy easter, he would not eat bread; his food instead was edible vegetables and moistened grain, and as a result of this, there was hardly any flesh upon him. Tears to him were sweet as honey, so that his eyes were deeply sunken, like holes in walls, and because of the great flow of tears continually streaming from his eyes like water, they had become very black. God was with him all his days.

**13.** When he was in his monastery, he would see a multitude of sins being committed throughout the whole world, and of those who came to him, he used to know all that they had thought and done. He would therefore pray for them all, so that they might be saved and find mercy at the tribunal of Christ.

**14.** Now it happened one day that a man who lived in the village of Psenkhōout in the nome of the city of Pšoi[17] came to my father, the prophet apa Shenoute. He came in very great anguish of heart, and he therefore sent [a message] into my father saying: 'O my holy father, I want to receive your blessing. It may be that by your holy prayers the mercy of God will come upon me so that God will forgive me my sins, for they are very many'. And the holy prophet apa Shenoute was told all that the man had said. My father said to the one that brought the message: 'Go and say to the man who has come: "If you will obey me in what I shall say to you, you will see me; if you will not obey me, you will not look upon my face".' The man said: 'I will obey you, my lord and father, in all that you command me'. So the holy apa Shenoute said: 'Bring him in to me'.

**15.** When he came in to my father, he fell down before him and greeted him, and my father apa Shenoute said to him: 'Declare your sin before us all so that you may go whither you will go'. The man said to him: 'I was sitting one day by the threshing-floor of my village when a man passed by me with a purse around his neck—I saw the leather strap round his neck. The man was riding his mule and urging it on. I seized my sword, ran after him, and killed him.

Straightaway I looked in the purse which was round his neck, for I thought I would find in it a great quantity of gold which I would take and use to enjoy myself for many days. In it I found one single coin.[18] I then dug [a hole] in the ground, buried him, and came here to you, my holy father. Tell me now what you want me to do so that the Lord might have mercy on me and forgive my sins.'

My righteous father and prophet apa Shenoute said to him: 'Do not stay here, but get up quickly and go into the city of Šmin, where you will find the duke.[19] He has come south down the river and is being greeted by his people.[20] Some thieves who robbed an eminent man of the city of Šmin will be handed over to him and he will be incensed with them. You too must go and join the thieves, and they will say to the duke: "He is here with us". The duke will ask you: "Is it true?" Say to him: "It is true", and he will therefore kill you with the others. You will then enter into the eternal life of God. **16.** The man left immediately and did just as the holy [apa Shenoute] had told him, and the duke cut off his head with the rest of the thieves. In this way the mercy of God came upon him, just as my father told us.

**17.** It happened on one occasion that the holy Cyril[21] sent for my father apa Shenoute the prophet and apa Victor the archimandrite[22] on account of the impious Nestorius,[23] and after they had entered the royal city,[24] our righteous father apa Shenoute was walking into the king's palace when he found a grain of wheat which had been thrown away. He picked it up and put it in the pouch in his [goat-] skin [habit] until he returned to his monastery. **18.** When the king had dismissed them so that they could go back to their [own] places, my father apa Shenoute went to board the ship with our holy fathers abba Cyril the archbishop and apa Victor the archimandrite, but because the lesser servants did not know him, they said to him: "You cannot go on board with the archbishop". My father said to them: 'If not, then the Lord's will be done!' Then he and his disciple who had gone with him went a short distance away and he stood in prayer, saying: 'My Lord Jesus Christ, how will you take me to my monastery?' While he was thinking these things to himself, behold! a shining cloud came down from heaven, lifted up both him and his disciple, snatched him up into the heights, and flew off with him. **19.** And when they reached the open sea, abba Cyril looked up and saw my father apa Shenoute with his disciple in the middle of the cloud, and cried out: 'Bless us, our holy father, the new Elijah!' My father apa Shenoute said to him: 'Remember me, O my holy father'. And in this way the cloud flew off with him and brought him to his monastery.

**20.** Now it was summertime there, and as the brothers were grinding [grain for] bread, he took the grain of wheat he had brought with him on his return from the king's palace, and threw it under the mill-stone; and the Lord sent so great an abundance[25] from the mill-stone that they were quite unable to gather it all up.[26] And because they were exhausted and unable to gather it up, the brothers complained. My holy father apa Shenoute went up to the mill-stone, laid his palm-branch upon it, and said: 'Mill-stone, I say to you, cease!' And it ceased immediately in accordance with the word of my father the righteous prophet apa Shenoute, truly the man of God, whose works are as powerful as those of the first prophets and the apostles. Innumerable are his good deeds and the miracles which he effected by the grace of the Holy Spirit which was ever in him.

**21.** Furthermore, when the holy archbishop Cyril had gone back to his city, he sent for my father apa Shenoute and asked him: 'When you were sitting on the cloud, how many days did it take you to reach your monastery?' My father apa Shenoute said to the archbishop: 'Forgive me, my holy father, I am unworthy of such a thing'. Abba Cyril said to him: 'I adjure you by the prayers of the saints to tell me what happened to you'. My father said to him humbly: 'Since you adjure me, I went to the monastery on the very day on which we talked together, you from the ship and I on the cloud, and on the evening of the same day I was at worship[27] with the brothers'. The holy archbishop Cyril and apa Victor the archimandrite were immediately astonished, and they therefore glorified God who alone works miracles in his saints who do his will and put their trust in him. After this, [our father apa Shenoute] left the archbishop and returned to his monastery.

**22.** One day our father apa Shenoute was sitting by an outcrop[28] of rock, and with him was our Lord Jesus Christ and they were talking together. Then my father the prophet said to him: 'My Lord, I would like to see a ship sailing here'. The Lord said to him: 'My chosen Shenoute, I will not cause you distress', and he parted from him. **23.** A short time thereafter, by the command of God the creator, the place was filled with water, and [God] caused a ship to come sailing by on the deep water which was there. The Lord himself took the form of the captain and some angels also took the form of the other sailors. It sailed on until it came to where the holy apa Shenoute was standing in prayer, and the Lord said to my father apa Shenoute: 'Take the rope!' He stretched out his hand and took the rope, but there was nothing to which he could tie it. Then he went to the overhanging outcrop of rock and grasped it with his finger and thumb. At that very moment, it was immediately pierced through, just like wax in front of a flame. He ran the rope through the stone and tied it, and that stone is pierced to this very day as an everlasting sign for all generations.

**24.** At one time they were working in the well which was being dug in the monastery, and the brothers were working there when the devil laid a trap for them: by his will, [the well] fell in on the labourers who were working there. One of the brothers who had been involved in the digging ran and told our father apa Shenoute. He arose, took his palm-branch, and went down to the well; he reached out with his palm-branch and drove it into the wall of the well. It immediately took root and sent up palm-branches and palm-leaves, and the men who were working ate its fruit. From that day to this, the well has never moved again.

**25.** It happened one day that our Saviour was sitting talking with my father apa Shenoute, and I, Besa, his disciple, came in wanting to meet him. The Saviour immediately withdrew. After I had come in and received a blessing from my father, I asked him: 'My holy father, who was that talking with you, and where did he go when I came in?' My father the prophet said to me: 'It was the Lord Jesus Christ who was with me just now, speaking mysteries to me'. I said to him: 'I, too, would like to see him so that he might bless me'. My father said to me: 'You will not be able to see him, because you are only a novice'.[29] I said to him: 'I am a sinner, my holy father'. He said to me: 'It is not so, but you are faint-hearted'.[30] Again, in tears, I said to him: 'I beg you, my father, let your mercy come upon me so that I, too, may be worthy to see him'. My father said to me: 'If you wait until the sixth hour tomorrow, come in [then], and you will find me sitting down with him. See that you say nothing at all!' **26.** On the following day, I came in accordance with my father's instruction and, as was the custom, knocked on the door-knocker so that I might go in and receive a blessing. Straightaway, the Lord departed from him. I wept and said: 'I am wholly unworthy to see the Lord in the flesh'. But my father said to me: 'He will comfort your heart, Besa, my son, and let you hear his sweet voice'. And that one time, though it was more than I deserved, I heard him speaking with my father, and I have been grateful to him all the days of my life.[31]

**27.** It happened once that there was a great drought, and the inhabitants of the nome of Šmin and those of the nome of Pšoi[32] came in a crowd to my father to be fed by him. My father gave them bread until the loaves ran out, and the brother who was in charge of the bread-store came to my father apa Shenoute and said: 'That was a great deal of bread, my father! What will you do [now] for the multitudes who have gathered to us and for the brothers?' In reply, my

father said to me and to the one who distributed the loaves:
'Go and gather up the remaining loaves together with [all]
the little fragments, moisten them, and give them to the
crowds to eat'. **28.** We, then, went off in accordance with
his word and gathered them up, and we left nothing behind.
We went [back] to him and told him: 'We have left nothing
behind', and he said to us: 'Pray to God that he will bring
about such a blessing that you can feed them all'. We did not
wish to disobey him, but instead went away, and when the
time came, we went to open the door of the breadstore, and
the abundance of God poured forth upon us while we were
[still] outside the door of the bread-store. In this way, the
multitudes ate, and when they were full they glorified God
and our father.

**29.** It happened once that the bakers complained about
the ashes they had to carry away. Our father knew this and
said to them: 'How many ovens are there?'. They said to him:
'There are eleven'. My father said to them: 'Go and throw
all the ashes which you normally bring from the ten ovens
into the one in the middle, and I trust[33] in God and the
prayers of the saints that it will never be filled up'. This they
did in accordance with his true word: all the ashes which they
brought from the ten ovens they packed into the one [in the
middle], and from that day to this it has not filled up.[34]

**30.** Before they had yet built the church, our Lord Jesus
Christ appeared to our father apa Shenoute and said: 'Arise,
and measure out the church and the foundation of the
monastery, and build a sanctuary in my name and yours'. My
father apa Shenoute said to the Lord: 'My Lord, where shall
I find anything to spend on the building of a sanctuary?' The
Saviour said to him: 'Arise and go to [your] dwelling-place
in the desert; pick up what you will find on the way and
spend it on the sanctuary. You may perhaps think it the
devil's doing: it is not. It is instead the means whereby you
may build the church and the monastery in accordance with
my will. I, the Lord, have spoken'. **31.** Our father, for

his part, then arose and went into the inner desert, and spent
the whole night there in prayer. But when he had left and
was on his way out of the desert in the morning, he found a
small leather bag [of gold?],[35] about a handsbreadth in
length, so he stretched out his hand, picked it up, and went
to the monastery. **32.** Thereupon, our Lord Jesus Christ
came to our father, and they went off together and laid out
the foundation of the sanctuary. My father then arranged for
the workmen and craftsmen, the stonemasons and the carpenters. They worked on the church, and with the Lord help-
ing them in all that they did with everything they needed,
they completed it.

**33.** It happened once that a man came to our father the
prophet. He was a man from Pemje[36] and he had with him a
hundred and twenty pieces of gold. Someone else, a friend
of his, came with him, and the man said to his friend: 'I want
to give a small gift to the sanctuary of apa Shenoute to be
given as alms for my salvation. However, I am not going to
hand them over until I know first whether the great man[37]
will give them as alms or not'. **34.** So he gave the gold
pieces to the other brother who had come with him, dressed
himself in clothes beneath his station, and entered the
monastery. He went to my father the prophet apa Shenoute
and spoke to him like this: 'I beg you, my holy father, have
mercy upon me and give me a small gift of just twenty
pieces of gold so that I can give them to the money-lender.
Otherwise, he will throw me out of my house and take it
from me'. My father said to him: 'This is no place to joke,
my son! Perhaps you would like another twenty pieces of
gold to add to the hundred and twenty which you brought
when you came because you would like to accumulate a
great number?' Then my father called a brother monk and
said to him: 'Go along a certain road to the field. You will
find a man sitting on the ground combing his hair[38] and
having a pitcher of water in his hand. Say to him: "Your
friend says, 'Just as I said to you "Sit here until I find out

whether the great man will give them as charity or not",
[I say] now, "Arise and come [to me]".' **35.** And when
the brother monk had gone off to the field as my father had
commanded him, he found the man and said to him the
words which my father had told him. The man who had
come to my father was standing before him in great
astonishment. Then he exclaimed: 'Truly, I know today that
there is a prophet in this monastery, just as I have seen it
with my own eyes'. After this, he gave the gold to my father
the prophet apa Shenoute, and after they had prayed, the
two of them departed from him in peace, glorifying God and
his saints.

**36.** One day there came a man from a foreign country. He
was from the village of Komentios,[39] and when he heard of
the miracles of our righteous father apa Shenoute, he came to
receive a blessing from him. My father replied to him like
this: 'How shall I bless you when you have committed a great
and most grievous sin?' The man replied to my father apa
Shenoute: 'I do not know what sin I have committed! I am a
Christian, and I have believed in the God of heaven since I
was a child.' My father said to him: 'Do you not remember
the day when you ate, drank, and slept in your house?
While you were sleeping, the enemy, the Devil, deceived you.
You got up, took your sword, went out, found a woman,
and slit open her belly with your sword'. The man replied:
'Truly, my holy father, what you say is true; yet if a sinful
man does penance, does he not receive forgiveness?' My
father the prophet replied to him: 'There is indeed repentance. If you endure the chastisement I shall give you, God
will forgive you, for God does not want the death of a sinner, but that he leave his wicked ways, do good, and live'.*
**37.** So as soon as the man heard these words of our father,
he cut his hair and donned the holy habit; struggling
gloriously, he was an outstanding monk to the day of his
death.

*Ezk 33:11

**38.** The third day after he had been made a monk, he filled a pitcher with water, and my father went with him into the inner desert until he was thirteen miles from the monastery. There he left him in a cave in a rock. The cave was circular, just as large as he was tall, and the door of the cave opened out above him like a window. **39.** My father apa Shenoute used to come to him once a week in order to visit him and bless him on Saturday and the Lord's day, and bring him what he needed for the week: a small pitcher of water and a small loaf of bread. **40.** A year after he had been made a monk, my father the prophet went in to him and said: 'What has happened to you? Tell me.' The man replied: 'Just when the night had given way to first light, I saw my body shaking so badly that I said: "All my sinews have been pulled from my body", and I was troubled, thinking that I would soon die. After this, behold! a form which stank dreadfully like a rotten corpse came out of my body; it went down a cleft in the rock like a smoky vapour, floated away, and disappeared. I myself was in a stupor until you called inside to me'. The holy prophet apa Shenoute replied: 'Be comforted, today salvation has come upon you and the Lord has forgiven your sin'. After this, my father took him and brought him back to the monastery among the brethren. **41.** Then I, Besa, the disciple of the holy old man, went to my father and said: 'Is this not the man from a foreign country who once came to us?' He said to me: 'It is'. I said to him: 'Where has he been all this time?' My father replied: 'After an evil beast had wounded him, I took him to the doctor. He healed him, and salvation came upon him'. The brother glorified God all his days.

**42.** One day, a man from the town of Šmin came to him. He was a notable businessman of very great wealth, and thieves had robbed his house, leaving him nothing. He came to my father and cried: 'Help me, my lord and father! They have devastated my house and left me nothing at all!'. My father apa Shenoute replied: 'Arise and go north to the

town of Siōout;⁴⁰ you will find three men sitting on the
ground outside the door of the city-gate, one of them will be
combing his hair. Say to him: "Shenoute says: Come to me
so that I may speak with you about a certain matter", and
the man will talk with you'. **43.** So after he had received
his blessing, the businessman departed and went north to the
town of Siōout, and he found the three men sitting on the
ground outside the city-gate, just as my father had told him,
and one of them was combing his hair. To him the businessman said: 'Friend, the man of God apa Shenoute says: Come
to me so that I may speak with you and tell you of this
matter'. The man said to him: 'Indeed! Behold, for many
days I have wanted to see that holy [man] to receive a blessing from him'. **44.** There and then the two of them arose
and set off together, and came to the holy apa Shenoute and
received his blessing. He said to them: 'Sit down for a little
while and rest'. **45.** After this, my father spoke with the
man he had sent for—he who had robbed the businessman's
house—and said to him: 'My son, go and give back to the man
the possessions which you stole and carried away, and I will
make him give you a few of them'. The man was afraid and
said to my father: 'My holy father, it was not I alone who
carried them off!' My father said to him: 'I know that too,
my son'. The man said to my father: 'If he will not tell anyone at all, I will take him and give him back his possessions
complete and intact'. **46.** Then my father called the businessman and made him take an oath, saying: 'I will never
reveal the matter to the day of my death'. So he took him
and gave him back all his possessions as they were, just as our
father apa Shenoute had commanded, and the businessman
gave him a small portion of his possessions and sent
him away.

**47.** Afterwards, the businessman came back again to our
father the prophet and received his blessing. My father apa
Shenoute said to him: 'Look, my son, you want to go to the
city of Alexandria;⁴¹ do me this favour: after you arrive, buy

the first thing you come across for sale and bring it to me. Whatever you give for it I will give to you when, by God's will, you return to me'.[42]  **48.**  On his way to Alexandria, the businessman arrived at Chereu,[43] and as soon as he disembarked from the ship, he found a man who had a silver portable-altar[44] which the man had stolen and carried off from one of the monasteries of our father apa Shenoute, the faithful man. When the businessman saw the altar he said to himself: 'If I buy this silver altar and take it to the great man of God, I will be ashamed to take anything from him, for he had pity on me, told me about my possessions, and had them given back to me. I will not buy it, lest I lose something else with my own hands!'[45]  **49.**  And when he went into the city of Alexandria and again met the man with the altar, he did not buy it. After another two days he once more met the man carrying the altar in everyone's presence, and again he did not buy it. When the businessman had sold his wares and went down to the river to board the ship, the man came again with the altar, and again he did not buy it.  **50.**  But one of the sailors on the ship which the businessman boarded bought it for four gold pieces, and he said to himself: 'I will take it to the sanctuary of apa Shenoute, the man of God'.

**51.**  When they arrived at their city, the sailor took the altar, brought it to the monastery, and offered it to my father, saying: 'My father, would you like to buy this portable-altar?' My father said to him: 'Indeed I would, but tell me how much you paid for it, my son'. The sailor said: 'I paid eight gold pieces for it, my father'. My father apa Shenoute said to him: 'No, my son, see that you do not lie; it was instead four gold pieces that you paid for it'. The sailor said to him: 'It is true; that is really what I paid for it. Take it, O my holy father'. My father said to him: 'My son, take five gold pieces for it'. But [the sailor] said to him: 'I will take nothing for it, my father. Remember me, my father, in your holy prayers'. And so, after he had received a blessing, he left my father and went to his house glorifying God.

**52.** After a month[46] had passed, that businessman—the one to whom my father gave back his possessions which had been stolen—came to the monastery. It was he to whom [my father] had said: 'Buy the first thing you come across for sale and bring it to me', but he had not bought it (I mean the altar which the sailor had bought for my father). The businessman said to my father: 'While I was out walking, I dropped a purse of gold, and I do not know where it fell'. Now it was actually the sailor who bought the altar who had found the purse of gold which he had dropped, and it contained sixty pieces of gold. But the businessman did not know this, and instead he entreated my father in tears, saying: 'Let your mercy come upon me!' My father apa Shenoute said to him: 'This is destiny; the riches of this world are like a prostitute: she is in your house today, but tomorrow she makes a contract with someone else.[47] Now, my son, God has given the gold you lost to whom he will, and you will never ever find it'. So the businessman went away with anguish in his heart and in great shame.

**53.** In a word, great signs and a multitude of miracles were worked by our father apa Shenoute, truly the true prophet and the bearer of the [Holy] Spirit. When they were spread abroad, they filled the face of the whole earth so that his renown even reached [the ears of] the pious[48] kings. They were told: 'There is a man in the south of Egypt called Shenoute. Whatever he says truly comes to pass'. And the king said: 'He is obviously a holy man of the Lord'.

**54.** So the king, who loved God, was not at all negligent, but instead wrote a letter to my father the prophet apa Shenoute written in this form:

*I, Theodosius the Younger,[49] an unworthy king to whom the Lord God has given the kingdom despite my unworthiness, write to you, O holy apa Shenoute, truly the man of God! I salute you, O my holy father, and beseech you to hasten to come to us, so that we and all my citizens might be*

*worthy of your blessing. The kingdom and the
entire senate*[50] *is looking forward to your holy
visit to us. So do not be negligent, our holy
father, but come to us. We thirst for you and your
holy teachings, according to the things which those
who have come to us tell us about the graces with
which God has favoured you. Remember us in
your holy prayers. Farewell in the name of the
holy Trinity.*

**55.** He sealed the letter and gave it to his personal
courier, who was called Eudoxius, and wrote another to the
duke of [the city of] Antinōou.[51] So the courier went to
Egypt, and when he had gone south, he entered the city of
Antinōou and gave the letters to the duke. They then arose
and came to the monastery of my father the holy apa
Shenoute, and after receiving his blessing, they sat down.
The courier then brought out the letters of the king and
presented them to my father apa Shenoute.

**56.** When [my father] received the letters and began to
read, he reached the passage where it was written: 'Make
haste to come to us in the royal capital'. He was then greatly
grieved and deeply afflicted in his heart, and said to the
courier: 'What does the king want with me? I am a monk
living in this monastery for the sake of God, praying and
supplicating for my sins'. The courier said to my father: 'My
lord and holy father, he wishes to enjoy your blessing'. My
father said to him: 'Look, perhaps you will be able to excuse
me, for truly, I am an old man'. The courier said to him: 'My
holy father, do not hinder this business. In truth, I will not
be able to obstruct the command of my lord the king'. Our
father the prophet said to him: 'Go [now] and rest for a
little while, you and the men who came with you, and take
[what you need] from the food which the brothers use'.

**57.** When they had been two days in the monastery the
courier entreated my father, saying: 'Arise and let us go, my
father, so that you will not bring down upon me a grave

threat on the part of my lord the king'. My father apa Shenoute said to him: 'Can you not excuse me, my son? Go in peace and say to the king: "The man is old and could not come with me".' The courier said to him: 'If you do not come willingly, then there are soldiers here who will take you there unwillingly!' My father the prophet said to him: 'In that case, grant me this day until tomorrow, and if God wills, we will go'. **58.** So after they had received a blessing, the courier and the duke and the whole party who were with them retired until the morning.

When evening came, our holy father apa Shenoute went into the sanctuary, stretched out his hands, and prayed to God that he would show him what he should do. And when he gave the 'amen', behold! a shining cloud snatched him up, flew away with him to the royal capital, and left him in the middle of the palace in the place where the king was; and there came a great light in the . . . .[52] where the king was sleeping. **59.** The king leaped up and said to my father: 'What sort of thing are you, for I am much disturbed!' My father apa Shenoute said: 'I am Shenoute the monk, for whom you sent. What do you want with me, a sinner, that you trouble your soldiers to fetch me, a feeble monk?' The king said to him: 'How did you get here, my holy father, and how many days were you on the journey?' My father said to the king: 'It was Christ Jesus, the son of the living God in whom we believe, together with his good Father and the Holy Spirit, who brought me here to you, so that I might satisfy you fully in what you have determined, and also to let you know that before I came here to you, I was at worship this very evening with the brothers in the monastery'. The king said to him: 'My holy father, where did you leave the courier and the soldiers I sent with him?' My holy father apa Shenoute replied and said to the king: 'I left them sleeping in the monastery'. The king, with great faith, said: 'Truly, before this day I had heard with my ears of the miracles of your holy and blessed paternity, but today I have seen them face to face!'

**60.**   Again my father said to him: 'And for what reason have you sent for me?' The king said to him: 'I sent for your holiness because I, together with the royal house and the whole city, want to enjoy your holy blessing and your blessed prayers'. My father said to him: 'May Jesus Christ bless you, O king who loves God, and all your city; may he establish your throne like that of your holy fathers Arcadius and Honorius;[53] may he perfect you all in the faith of your fathers, confirming and guarding the precepts and faith of our fathers the apostles'.

**61.**   The king said to my father: 'Stay with us a few days, my holy father, so that we may enjoy you to the full'. My father said to him: 'It is necessary for me to go. Of your charity, write a letter in your name which I can give to the courier so that he and those with him may return to you in peace, and not trouble me in trying to bring me to you yet again'.   **62.**   Then Theodosius the king wrote a letter in this form:

> I, Theodosius the king, write to Eudoxius the courier: as soon as you receive these letters from our father the prophet apa Shenoute, the priest, monk, and archimandrite, who, in a way which God [alone] knows, came to me this very night to the place where I sleep, make haste to return, and do not try again to bring him to us.

He also wrote to him on certain other secret matters which were just between the king and the courier, sealed [the letter] with his ring, and gave it to our father. Him he embraced, and after he had received his blessing, sent him away in peace.   **63.**   Thereupon, the cloud again lifted up my father and took him to the monastery the same night, and that same night, before the break of day, he was at worship with the brothers in the monastery. And no-one knew that he had gone to the king and returned to his monastery.

**64.**   When morning came, the courier said to my holy

father the superior:[54] 'Of your charity, arise and let us go, so that you do not bring upon me a grave offence and the anger of my lord the king'. My father said to the courier: 'Look, my son, will you go to the king and say to him: "He is an old man"?' The courier said to him: 'If you do not come willingly, I will take you against your will'. **65.** When my father realised that he would take him by force and that he would not go back [to the king] leaving him there, he then put his hand in his habit, brought out the king's letter and handed it to the courier. When the latter took it and looked it over, he recognized it as the king's, and looked at the face of my holy father apa Shenoute. My father said to him: 'Open it and read it!' And when he began to read it and came upon the matters which were a secret between himself and [the king], he went out of his mind. My father immediately made the sign [of the cross] over him until he regained his senses, and he then read the whole [of the letter]. When he had finished reading it, he straightaway threw himself down at my father's feet and said: 'Truly, my lord and father, you are a man whose feet should not be allowed to tread the unclean earth!' **66.** And he said to him: 'I would like to stay with you and become a monk'. My father said to him: 'No, my son; arise and go to the king instead, for he is asking for you, you and your soldiers'. The courier said to him: 'Of your charity, my holy father, bless me with your holy mouth, O strong disciple and dwelling-place of God!' So my father blessed him, saying: 'May the Lord Jesus Christ bless you and deliver you from the snares of the devil, and may you inherit the good things which endure forever'. **67.** And so he left our father and went his way to the king, taking with him the letter which my father had brought when he returned from the royal seat; and it was a strength and comfort to him all his life.

**68.** It happened one day that some of the great men of the city of Šmin came to him because they wanted to receive his blessing, and with them also came certain monks of great renown from Šiēt,[55] who wanted to hear his words. The latter said to him: 'Our holy father, will there be a monk in this generation the like of the blessed Antony[56] ?' **69.** My righteous father said to them: 'Even if all the monks of this time came [together] in a single place, they would not make a single Antony!' The brothers and notables of the city were amazed at the saying of our father the prophet, and so, when they had received his blessing, they went away glorifying God.

**70.** One day, our father and our Lord Jesus were sitting down talking together. Just then, behold! the bishop of the city of Šmin passed by the monastery. He wanted to go to Alexandria to pay his respects to the archbishop,[57] and before travelling north, he wanted to visit my father. He sent in a request to my father saying: 'Make haste to come [forth] so that I can meet you [and discuss] this small matter with you before I travel north'. Now at that time, as I said earlier, my father was sitting with the Saviour, so he said to the servant: 'Go and say to him: he says, "I am not free at the moment".' The servant went back and reported these words to the bishop. **71.** The bishop again said to the servant: 'Say to him: Of your charity, come [forth] so that I can meet you!' The old man said to him through the brother: 'Say to him: I am not free at the moment'. And the servant reported this to the bishop. **72.** The bishop was annoyed and said to the servant: 'Say to him: If you do not come, you are excommunicated!' The servant went to our father and said to him what the bishop had told him. But my father smiled graciously with laughter and said: 'See what this man of flesh and blood has said! Behold, here sitting with me is he who created heaven and earth! I will not go while I am with him.' Then the Saviour said to my father: 'O Shenoute, arise and go out to the bishop, lest he excommunicate you. Otherwise, I will not let you enter [heaven] because of the covenant I made with Peter, saying: "What you will bind on earth will be bound in heaven, and what you will

loose on earth will be loosed in heaven".'* And when my
father heard these words of the Saviour, he arose, went out
to the bishop and greeted him. When they finished their discussion, the bishop departed from my father apa Shenoute
in the peace of God. Amen.

**73.** One day, when my father was sitting in the monastery, behold! the devil and a host of other demons with him
came in and spoke to my father with great threats and
wickedness. When my father saw the devil, he recognised
him immediately, and straightaway he sprang upon him and
grappled with him. He seized him, hurled him to the ground
and placed his foot on his head, and shouted to the
brothers who were nearby: 'Seize the others who followed
him!' And they immediately vanished away like smoke.[58]

**74.** It happened one day that apa Martyrius of Phbōou[59]
was going to go to Constantinople to the king, Theodosius,
and when he arrived in the neighborhood[60] of the monastery,
he said: 'Before I travel north, I want to go and pay my
respects to my father the prophet apa Shenoute'. A young
monk called John, who was secretary to the old man apa
Martyrius, replied obstinately: 'What prophet? Let us move
on! For in truth, he does not even know what he ate this
evening!' After this, he disembarked[61] and he and his father
went on their way, but when [apa Martyrius] drew near the
monastery, my father arose and came out to him. Then,
when they had greeted each other, he took them into the
monastery, and when they had prayed, they sat down.
**75.** Straightaway my father the prophet apa Shenoute spoke
thus: 'Where is John?', and the brothers looked at each
other. Then he said: 'It is you, John, to whom I am speaking,
the secretary of the old man apa Martyrius'. Then my father
seized him and said to him: 'Truly, John, Shenoute does not
know what he ate this evening, but on the day of judgement,
this miserable body which is now talking to you will sit down

---

*Mt 16:19

with the apostles to judge with them.* Henceforth, see that
you do not mistrust God and his servants!' The young man
immediately threw himself down at the feet of my holy
father and besought him, saying: 'Forgive me; I have sinned!',
and after this, the old man apa Martyrius departed from my
father, glorifying God and amazed at what had happened.
    **76.** It happened once that our father the prophet apa
Shenoute went to the royal court, to the pious kings, because of the oppressions which the rulers were inflicting upon
the poor. When he entered the city, the whole town was in a
turmoil because of his visit to them, and they were all coming
to him, those from the palace and those from the whole city,
receiving his blessing with great faith, and each and every one
of them bringing him into their houses so that he would pray
there. **77.** One day, then, when he was wending his way
to the house of one of the [men] held in honour by the king
in order to pray there, the day had begun to decline and the
time for the brothers with him to eat their bread had passed.
They were then complaining, saying: 'Our father will kill us
like this; we want to drink a little water!' For it was summer
time, and those who have been to Constantinople tell of the
very high temperatures which often occur there. Our father
apa Shenoute knew in the spirit what they were thinking,
and while he was walking with them along a street, he
touched a certain door. **78.** It opened on the instant, and
when he had gone in, he called the brothers who were walking with him and said: 'Come in and eat'. And when they
went in they found a dining room all prepared: the table laid
out in exactly the fashion of their monastery, and everything
they needed was laid out with the bread; and there were two
young monks standing there with little pitchers ready to give
them water and whatever else they needed. So he said to the
brothers: 'Sit down and eat', and after they had eaten, they
arose and left. **79.** They said to him: 'Our father, who pre-

---

*Cf. Mt 19:28

pared this dining room, and who were those two brothers who were serving us? Truly, we would hardly find what we needed like this in our own monastery!' He said to them frankly: 'Give glory to God, for he who sent food to Daniel in the lion's den* is also he who now, today, prepared this dining room for you, and those two brothers who were serving you are angels of the Lord'. The brothers were amazed, and glorified God and our father.

**80.** It happened that when our father apa Shenoute was sitting in the presence of the king, behold! a notable senator[62] who was held in high honour by the king came to my father, wishing to receive his blessing. He greeted him and came to take his hand to kiss it. My father drew his hand back from him and would not give it to him. The king said to him: 'My holy father, of your charity, give him your blessing, for he is a great [man] both in the palace and in the whole senate'. Our father was saddened and said angrily: 'Do you want me to give my hand to a man who defiles the temple of God with his abominable works?' Then the king was amazed, and glorified God and his holy prophet apa Shenoute.

**81.** On another occasion, our holy father apa Shenoute arose and went to the city of Šmin to chastise a pagan because of the oppressions he was inflicting on the poor. He [went] to find him and threaten him with the evils which God would bring upon his head, and when he found him, he spoke to him in these [terms]. He, however, being truly impious, stretched out his hand (which deserved to be cut off) and punched our father apa Shenoute in the face. **82.** At the very moment he hit him, behold! someone who was coming along the streets of the city inspiring as much fear as a great king came up to the impious one and seized his hair. He punched him in the face and, followed by a huge crowd, dragged him through the whole city until he reached the

*Cf. Dn 14:32-38

river. He dragged him down to the water, and the two of them plunged in and were never seen again. Everyone who had seen them, therefore, said: 'This is the power of God which he sent to take swift vengeance on that impious pagan because of the many oppressions he was inflicting upon us'. And so they glorified God who works miracles by the hands of his chosen ones.

**83.**   Another time, our holy father apa Shenoute arose to go to the village of Pleuit[63] in order to throw down the idols which were there. So when the pagans came to know of this, they went and dug in the place which led to the village and buried some [magical] potions [which they had made] according to their books because they wanted to hinder him on the road. **84.**   Our father apa Shenoute mounted his donkey, but when he began to ride down the road, as soon as the donkey came to a place where the potions had been buried, it would stand still and dig with its hoof. Straight-away the potions would be exposed and my father would say to the servant: 'Pick them up so that you can hang them round their necks'. Time and time again the servant who was going with him would beat the donkey, saying: 'Move!' But my father would say to him: 'Let him be, for he knows what he is doing!', and again  he would say to the servant: 'Take the vessels and keep them in your hand until we enter the village so that we can hang them round their necks'. When he entered the village, the pagans saw him with the magical vessels which the servant had in his hands. They immediately fled away and disappeared, and my father entered the temple and destroyed the idols, smashing them one on top of the other.

**85.**   On a later occasion, there was an island in the western part of the river planted with vineyards. They called it the island of Panehēou,[64] and it lay within sight of the city of Šmin. The owners of these vineyards were pagans who each year forced on the farmers the rotten wine of the island, extorting from them by violence what was not theirs. These farmers arose, went to the monastery, asked for my holy father the prophet apa Shenoute, and told him of the oppressions the men were inflicting upon them and of the distress they were in. My father the prophet said to them: 'Arise and go, and God will determine your judgement'.

**86.** During the night, our father the prophet apa Shenoute arose and went over to that island in the water with the vineyards planted on it, and struck the soil of the island a blow with the little palm branch he had in his hand and said: 'O island of Panehēou, I say to you, go into the middle of the river and sink down for ever, so that the poor will cease to suffer because of you'. Straightaway the island with vineyards and farms crossed over and went into the middle of the river, and before dawn had broken, the waters covered them and ships were sailing over them. In this way, the name of God was glorified by our holy father apa Shenoute the righteous.

**87.** It happened one time that there was a feast day in the monastery [in commemoration] of our fathers, and when some clerics and cantors had entered the monastery, they came to my father apa Shenoute and asked him for a little wine. He then gave them what they needed. After this, they asked him for some other things, and he gave them to them gladly. Again, in the same way, they repeated their request insatiably, and he gave to them again for the third time. Those who were sitting by him were amazed at his generosity, and said: 'If they continue to ask you, will you continue to give to them?' He said to them: 'I will; but they will go on drinking only the things which are here, because they have no hope of another life'.[65] *

**88.** It happened once that there was a pagan whose name was Gesios. He was very impious and used to blaspheme Christ, speaking profanities about him in his foolishness and his evil wickedness. When our righteous father came to know

---

*Cf. Tt 3:7

of his profanities, he cursed him, saying: 'His tongue shall be bound to the big toe of his foot in hell!' And this is what was done to him after he had died. My father testified to us and said: 'I saw him in hell with his tongue bound to the big toe of his foot, tormented without forgiveness because of his impiety'.

**89.** It happened one time that the Blemmyes came north, captured some of the cities, and took captive the men and their beasts of burden.[66] They went south with all that they had captured and camped in the nome of Psoi. Then my father apa Shenoute wanted to go to them for the sake of the captives they had captured, and when he crossed the river to go east to them, those he met first raised high their spears intending to kill him. Their hands immediately became stiff and dry like wood, fixed unbendably at full stretch, and they were crying out in great distress. The same thing happened in a similar way to the rest of these people until [my father] arrived at the seat of their king. **90.** When the latter realized that they could not overcome the power which was with him, he arose and bowed to the ground before him, saying: 'I beg you, restore my men's hands!' And when he made the sign [of the cross] over them, their hands were immediately restored to health. When the king promised him gifts, he did not take them, but when he spoke to him said only this: 'Give me the men; take for yourself all the spoils'*; and the king freely gave all of them to him. He crossed over to the west bank of the water with them and brought them to the monastery. He provided them with expenses and sent them away in peace, each to his own house, glorifying God and his holy prophet apa Shenoute.

**91.** It happened one day that when they were summoned to worship at the evening hour and the brothers were assembled in the church, someone else came behind them who was dressed in a royal robe and very beautiful in form. As soon as our holy father the prophet apa Shenoute saw him, he approached the one who was coming to him, spoke

*Gn 14:21*

to him with great reverence, took his hand, and led him up to the place in the church from which the brothers gave the recitation.[67] [The stranger] then gave the recitation sweetly and with great dignity, and all who heard him were delighted with his discourse, his pronunciation, and his outstanding learning. When he had finished the recitation, he walked into the sanctuary and disappeared. **92.** Some of the brothers then complained, saying: 'Could our father not find one of us to give the recitation apart from this layman whom he led up and who gave the recitation to the brothers?' When our father the prophet apa Shenoute knew that the brothers were complaining and thinking these things, he openly revealed the mystery to them and said to them: 'Believe me, my brothers, the man who went up and gave us the recitation just now is the holy prophet David, the son of Jesse; it was he who wanted to give the recitation in your church, and behold! the Lord favoured us with these great goods'. The brothers immediately rushed together into the sanctuary, thinking that they would find him and receive from him his blessing and teaching, but they saw no-one. Then they were all amazed at the way in which God had glorified the holy and great prophet, our father apa Shenoute.

**93.** One day, apa Martyrius, the archimandrite of Phbōou,[68] came north to visit and greet the prophet apa Shenoute. A certain cantor came with apa Martyrius, and when they came into the church to receive a blessing, the cantor stood up to sing, and without understanding the mystery, he [sang] on and on beyond all measure. Then the holy apa Martyrius said to our father the prophet apa Shenoute: 'My father, do you want to put an end to the cantor's singing? You see that the people and the brothers have received the blessing'. But my father said to him in reply: 'Why are you concerned about him? Let him sing! Behold, there is a choir of angels around him responding to him. Look, there is the prophet David standing at his side and giving him the words which need to be said'. And apa Martyrius was

amazed at the spirit of God which was in our father apa
Shenoute.

**94.**   It happened one day that our father the prophet apa
Shenoute was walking with the great prophet Jeremiah (in
the spirit? God knows! In body? Again, God knows!),* and
finally he came upon a brother who was lying down with his
head covered by his habit and reciting the words of Jeremiah
the prophet. Then holy Jeremiah stood over that brother
who was lying down reciting and wept until his tears flowed
down upon the brother who was lying down. My father
immediately roused the brother, saying: 'Get up quickly!',
and when he had got up, he asked him: 'Do you know the
source of these drops of water which are dripping over you?'
The brother said to him: 'I do not, but I suppose it rained'.
My father said to him openly: 'Believe me, my son, these
drops of water which have fallen upon you are the tears of
the prophet Jeremiah. When you were reciting his words just
now, he was standing over you weeping, because you were
not speaking them with heartfelt ardour.'

**95.**   Another time, our holy father was walking with the
prophet Ezekiel, and one of the brothers was sitting by himself reciting the words of the prophet. The holy prophet
Ezekiel went up to the brother and stood over him. The
brother who was reciting did not know this, and my father
apa Shenoute said to the prophet Ezekiel: 'Come and be
seated; do not weary yourself with standing'. The prophet
said to him: 'Leave me for a while. I will not pass by this
brother, for his recitation of my words truly strikes
home'.[69]

**96.**   There was also another brother sitting in a corner
reciting the twelve minor prophets, and as often as he would
recite them, beginning each one in order, our father apa
Shenoute would see the prophet he was reciting standing by
the brother until he finished the recitation. He would then

---

*Cf. 2 Co 12:2

leave and sit by our father apa Shenoute and the prophet Ezekiel. Now when the brother had finished eleven of the minor prophets and came to the last, that is, Malachi, because he was a man still subject to the flesh, he began to doze. And for a little while, sleep weighed down upon him since he had spent the whole night awake in his recitation. But the holy prophet Malachi did not cease standing over him. **97.** Then the prophet Ezekiel said to our father apa Shenoute: 'Trouble yourself to wake the brother so that he can finish the words of our brother Malachi. Then he too may come and sit down with us'. Our father went and woke him, saying: 'Rise up, my son, and let the great man leave, so that he will cease to be wearied on your account and may join his brothers'. So he arose and finished [the recitation]. Thereupon the prophet greeted his fellow prophets, and they departed from [our father].

**98.** It happened once that a brother erred in a certain matter—he was, after all, a man, and God alone is without sin—and our father apa Shenoute expelled him from the monastery in accordance with the Rule.[70] This brother went off into the desert weeping in great misery, but when he remembered God's mercies, he gave himself up to repentance and did penance, saying: 'Lord God, compassionate lover of mankind, who desires that none of the works of his hands should perish,* if today you so move the heart of my father that he forgives me what I did and receives me back again, it is my hope that I shall come to you having pleased you in everything'. **99.** At that very moment, while these words were still in his mouth, there appeared standing beside him an angel of the Lord who asked him: 'Why are you so distressed?' The brother replied: 'My brother, I am distressed because my holy father apa Shenoute has expelled me from the midst of the brethren, and I do not know what I shall do, except despair of my salvation. From this moment, I have no

---

*Cf. 2 P 3:9

hope of repentance'. The angel said to him: 'If your father were to receive you back again, will you observe the covenant which you made with God and carry out to the full what you have just promised?' Straightaway the brother fell at the angel's feet and said: 'Certainly, my lord! If his mercy falls upon me, it is my hope to observe these things and carry them out'. (For as we understood it from him, the angel was wearing a monk's habit at the time he appeared to the brother.) **100.** The angel said to him: 'Arise and go to him, and he will receive you'. The brother said to [the angel]: 'Those on guard at the gate will not permit me to go in to him'. The angel said to him: 'Get you gone; you will find no-one at the gate. Go in quickly, and you will find your father sitting at the entrance in front of the door of the church. Say to him: "He who just now stopped talking with you on the right of the altar says: Take me back again".'

**101.** Strengthened by this discourse, the brother arose and went to the monastery, and found no-one at the door, just as the angel had said to him. He went in immediately and found our father the prophet apa Shenoute sitting at the entrance of the church wearing a newly washed habit, for it was the Lord's day there and the hour for offering up the sacrifice to the Lord.[71] And when the brother began to tell our father the prophet apa Shenoute what he had heard from the holy angel, our father called the brother who was appointed to summon [the brethren] and said to him: 'Go and call to me the house-master[72] who expelled this brother'. When he came, our father said to him: 'Take in the brother so that he may stay with the brethren as before'. And the brothers, who did not know of the mystery which had occurred, were all amazed.

**102.** It happened one year that [the Nile] did not flood,[73] and our father apa Shenoute knew from God the hidden reason for it. He also revealed the matter to the brothers with his tears flowing from his eyes, and said to us: 'Pray to God. I, too, will go into the desert and spend this week praying to the Lord. See that no-one at all comes to me'. **103.** Then, after he had gone into the desert, someone arrived: on the fourth day of that week the duke came to the monastery wanting to pay his respects to our holy father apa Shenoute and receive his blessing. He called me, the lowly Besa, the disciple of our father, and said to me: 'I want to meet the holy old man and pay my respects to him'. I replied: 'He is not in this monastery, but has gone into the inner desert'. The duke again said to me: 'Go and call him to me'. The brothers replied: 'He said to us: Let no-one at all come to me for the whole of this week'. But the duke, being a man of importance, swore [an oath], saying: 'I will remain here with you, eating your provisions, until you go and call him to me so that I may receive his blessing'. **104.** After he had taken his ease in the abundance of the monastery for three days, we were in evil straits, and we therefore went into the desert to where our father the prophet was staying. When we knocked, he answered us with difficulty after a long time. Then he came out and was angry with us, and said: 'Did I not say to you: Let no-one come to me for the whole of this week?' Then we said to him: 'Forgive us, our holy father, the duke came to the monastery with his whole guard of soldiers, and it was he who forced us to come to you'. **105.** He, for his part, said to us: 'You know that I said to you that God has commanded that there should be no flooding of the land this year. Behold, then, I prayed to him, and he, as the good and merciful God, promised me that this year again he would cause the waters to come and cover the face of the land'. **106.** So when we asked him, he came with us to the duke. When the duke saw our father, he greeted him, and when he had received his blessing, he said to him: 'My father, do you want me to go south and wage war on the barbarians?'[74] [My father] said: 'Indeed I do!' The duke said to him: 'Let your mercy come upon me, my holy father, and give me one of your leather girdles to be a blessing for me'. And he gave it to him.

**107.** When the duke went south, he forgot to tie round him the girdle of our holy father, and when he went against the barbarians, they struck him down and killed many of his soldiers a first time and then again a second. Finally he came to his senses and said: 'Am I not stupid? I have not tied round me the leathern girdle which the old man the prophet apa Shenoute gave me.' He immediately tied it round him, went against the barbarians, and slaughtered them unsparingly. **108.** He then looked up into the sky and saw our father apa Shenoute in the middle of a shining cloud with a flaming sword in his hands, killing the barbarians. And the duke, too, went up into the cloud by the side of our father apa Shenoute and in this way he smote the barbarians with great ruin. Afterwards, the duke returned north offering thanks to God and to our holy father the prophet apa Shenoute, the righteous man.

**109.** There were two brothers lying sick in the monastery. One of them was zealous and watched over himself carefully; the other was very negligent, spending his days in vain pursuits. Now one day, it happened that our father apa Shenoute came to the place where they were sick to visit them. **110.** When he came to the negligent brother he said to him: 'Look at you! I see you suffering and near to death: what do you think of yourself?' The brother replied: 'Believe me, my father, I never ever performed a single one of your commands, and I do not know in what way I can justify myself'. **111.** Then he also went to the place where the righteous brother was, whose illness was not serious, and asked him: 'What do you think? If the Lord should visit you, are you confident now that you would find mercy?'. The latter replied: 'Believe me, my holy father, I was zealous in keeping all your commands, but if God is not merciful,* I do not know what will happen to me'. My father said to him: 'Good!'. **112.** After this, the zealous

---

*Cf. Ps 130:4

brother died and went to the Lord. The one who was negligent, however, recovered from his illness, but still persisted in his negligence, and our father apa Shenoute was saddened because of him. **113.** Now when the brothers were putting earth on the threshing-floor where they spread out the bread,[75] some of the brothers were carrying earth, and among them too was the negligent brother who had been restored from sickness. He was walking slowly with the basket of earth, idly cracking jokes and roaring with laughter. Our father the old man arose in anger, seized him, and threw him to the ground. He piled on top of him his basket of earth and spoke to him like this: 'Is it not enough for you that for your sake I gave up the zealous brother? I had you sent back since I wanted you to repent! And look, you have still paid no heed to your shameful works!' The brother arose and fell down before our father, saying: 'Forgive me!'. **114.** He went away and henceforth gave himself up to penance with great zeal and groanings and tears until the days of a month[76] had passed by. At the end of the month he fell sick and was dying, and our holy father apa Shenoute went in to him to visit him, and stayed at his side until he died. Then our father said to the brothers: 'Behold! Today a brother went to the Lord; in his life there is no decrease'.

**115.** One day, our Lord Jesus Christ came to our father apa Shenoute and spoke with him like this: 'Since your friends, the ascetics in the desert, are longing to see your sons, behold! they are coming to you tonight', and when he had said this, he withdrew from him. **116.** Then our father the prophet apa Shenoute assembled the senior brothers[77] and the housemasters in the monastery and spoke to them like this: 'There are some monks coming to us tonight. If they should come among you, see that no-one among you or among the brothers speaks with them. Instead, bow down your heads to them and receive their blessing, for they are truly holy men'. **117.** So when they had been summoned to assemble that night for the recitation (for it was winter, and they were sitting by the fire at night reciting by heart), behold! our father apa Shenoute came in, and with him in great glory walked three monks. When the brothers saw them, they all arose, paid their respects to them and received their blessing. After this, these holy [men] withdrew again, and with them went our holy father the prophet apa Shenoute.

**118.** When it was morning we gathered to him and asked him: 'Our father, who were those honourable men who came to us last night? We have not seen their like. They walked with majesty and wisdom, and their garments were glorious. They were different from other living men,[78] but were like angels of God'. Our father apa Shenoute said in reply: 'Go and give glory to God for the gift we have received. Believe me, these holy men who came to you last night were John the Baptist, Elijah the Tishbite, and Elisha. These great prophets longed to see you at your work and asked God [if they might do so]; behold! he sent them to you, and the saying which is written—"Things into which angels long to look"*—has been fulfilled among you'.

**119.** It happened one day that our father the prophet apa Shenoute went north to the mountain of Siōout to visit his friend the prophet apa John, the holy anchorite who was also called the Carpenter.[79] He lived secluded in the desert, shut up in a little cell,[80] and used to talk to those who went to him through a little window. **120.** To the north of the mountain of Siōout there are martyrs laid, their bodies buried in the road,[81] and every time he went north along the road, these martyrs would come forth before him before he reached the road where they lay and speak with him in greeting, saying: 'Welcome, beloved of God!'. Then they would walk with him, escorting him with great gladness for more than a mile, and bestowing upon him great honour. **121.** Many times, too, he spoke with our Lord Jesus Christ face to face. Again, he would sometimes speak with the

---

*1 P 1:12

prophets; sometimes the apostles would appear and speak with him. All the saints would speak with him and comfort him. Sometimes the angels would appear to him and tell him what he should say, whether in comforting [people] or in reproving them.

**122.** It happened one time that our father apa Shenoute was in the cell in the desert, and he delayed his return to the monastery because he was praying in those days for the river to flood.[82] He gave us a command, saying: 'Let no-one come into the desert'. **123.** So when something was needed for the monastery, we were afraid to send to him. Now there was a second [-in-command][83] set under our father, and the second called apa Joseph, our father's secretary, and said to him: 'Go up and tell our father of the matter and ask him what we should do'. He obeyed him and went up to our father to the cell in the desert. When he drew near the cell, it sounded to him as if [our father] was speaking to some people, and he was afraid to approach him. **124.** After a short time, our father called out and said: 'Come in, Joseph! Do not stay outside'. So he went in and received his blessing. My father said to him: 'Why did you come into the desert and not open the door of the cell and come in?'. He replied humbly: 'I thought that the rulers of the city had come up here to you and were talking with you. That was why I did not come in, my father'. Our father apa Shenoute replied to him and said: 'Joseph, Shenoute does not speak with men in the desert; it is the angels I speak with, or the prophets, or apostles, or martyrs. Nevertheless, Joseph, you lost a great blessing today, for the twelve apostles had come to visit me here and they just now arose and withdrew. Believe me, it was they who were speaking with me just now'.

**125.** One day, our father went to the city of Šmin to carry off in secrecy by night the idols in Gesios'[84] house. He then mounted his donkey together with two brother monks who were also mounted on beasts. During the night they went down to the river, and by divine providence they crossed the river without any ship or sailor, and entered the city. **126.** When they came to the pagans' door, the doors of the house opened immediately one after another until they entered the place where the idols were. So with the brothers who were with him, he picked them up, took them down to the river, smashed them in pieces and threw them in the river. **127.** Then again, in the same way, he and the brothers went back to the western bank of the river without ship or sailor; and moreover, that night none of the beasts made any noise at all until they had returned to the monastery. All of us were glorifying God and our father apa Shenoute for all the good things which he and our father were doing.

**128.** It happened on one occasion that our holy fathers convened a synod to anathematise the impious Nestorius, and my father the prophet apa Shenoute was also there together with the holy Cyril, the archbishop of Alexandria.[85] When they went into the church to set out the seats and sit down, they set out in the middle of the assembly another seat and placed upon it the four holy gospels. When the impious Nestorius came in with a great display of pride and shamelessness, he then picked up the four holy gospels, placed them on the ground, and sat down in the chair. **129.** When my father apa Shenoute saw what Nestorius had done, he leaped quickly to his feet in righteous anger in the midst of our holy fathers, seized the gospels, picked them up from the ground, and struck the impious Nestorius on his chest, saying: 'Do you want the Son of God to sit on the ground while you sit on the chair?'. In reply, the impious Nestorius said to my father apa Shenoute: 'What business do you have in this synod? You yourself are certainly not a bishop, nor are you an archimandrite or a superior, but only a monk!'. Our father replied and said to him: 'I am he whom God wished to come here in order to rebuke you for your iniquities and reveal the errors of your impiety in scorning the sufferings of the only-begotten Son of God, which he endured for us so that he might save us from our sins. And it is he who will now pronounce upon you a swift judgement!'. At that very moment [the impious Nestorius] fell off his chair to the ground, and in the midst of the synod of our fathers, he was possessed by the devil. **130.** There and then, the holy Cyril arose, took the head of our father apa Shenoute and kissed him. He took the stole[86] which was around his neck and placed it round the neck of apa Shenoute. He put in his hand his staff, and made him an archimandrite. And all who were present at the synod cried out: 'Worthy, worthy, worthy archimandrite!'.

**131.** There was a young boy[87] in the monastery who was a monk, and he was being much obstructed by childish thoughts. So because these demonic thoughts were tormenting him like this, he made a resolve in his heart and said: 'If my father should come to the door to visit me, I will go back with him into the world'. **132.** When our righteous father apa Shenoute knew of the brother's thoughts, he called him to him and said: 'Is it true that if your father comes, you will go back with him into the world?'. The boy laughed, and our father said to him: 'Truly, I will send you to your true father'. And when he had said this, he sent him away. **133.** The young boy began to sicken, and our father apa Shenoute was told about it. The brothers then asked him to pray for him so that he might recover, for he was truly in great pain. Our father the prophet said to them: 'What concern is he of yours? He wants to go to his father!'. When the brothers heard this, they withdrew. On the Saturday, which was the seventh day after the young boy became ill, he fell asleep at the ninth hour of the day. They wrapped him in a shroud, took him out, and buried him. **134.** When they had finished burying him, our father apa Shenoute assembled all the brothers and spoke to them with the word of God, saying: 'Believe me, brothers, behold! today there went to God a soul in whom there is no stain. Instead, it will go without any hindrance into the places of rest until it worships before the holy veil'. When the brothers heard this, they glorified God and prepared themselves to serve the Lord patiently and unswervingly.

**135.** It happened on another occasion that the governor[88] came south intending to go to war with the barbarians, and when he arrived before the monastery he sent [someone] to my father asking him to come over the river to him so that he could pay his respects to him and receive his blessing before going to war with the barbarians. He believed that if only he saw him, he would vanquish all his enemies. Our father arose and quickly went to him. **136.** Two ferocious lions which a certain man used to keep were tied to the boat, but when our father went to the boat to board it, the lions then bowed down their heads to him as if to receive his blessing. The governor and all those with him were amazed and said: 'Truly, this is a holy prophet!'. **137.** After this, the governor asked [our father] to give him his girdle as a blessing, so that he could tie it round him when he went to war with the barbarians, and he gave it to him. In this way he went south, fought with the barbarians, and smote them by means of the prayers of our holy father apa Shenoute, the man of God. After this, he returned north with those who were with him, glorifying God for the victory which he had gained by the prayers of our blessed father.

**138.** One day, our father the prophet apa Shenoute was engaged in their worship at night, and after he had completed the worship he rested for a little while and saw an apparition sent by the Lord. It was like this: he saw standing before him a man wholly filled with great glory. There was a great fragrance coming forth from his mouth and his face shone with light like the sun. The old man said to him: 'Who are you, my lord, surrounded as you are by this great glory?' The shining figure replied: 'I am Paul, the apostle of Christ. Because you love charity and give alms to anyone that asks you and keep all the commandments in all ways because of the love [of God], behold! the Lord has sent me to you to comfort you because of what you do for the poor and the destitute'. And he stayed talking with him like this until it was time to assemble in the church at night. **139.** [The apostle] then presented him with a loaf of bread and gave it to him. The old man took it and tied it in his scrip. The apostle said to him: 'Take this loaf and put it in the bread-store from which the brothers distribute the bread. Many holy men have blessed this loaf, and even our Lord Jesus Christ himself blessed it and made the sign [of the cross] over it. Now be strengthened and fortified; do not be afraid! The peace of God shall abide and remain with you forever'. He then greeted him once more and went away from him. **140.** The holy old man apa Shenoute arose from the vision and found the loaf tied in his scrip, and he glorified God, saying: 'How shall I repay the Lord for all that he has done for me?'.* Straightaway, he went out to go to the church with the brothers, and [on the way] went to the place from which the brothers distributed the bread. Then secretly, without letting anyone know, he took the blessed loaf which the apostle had given him in the vision and put it in the store-room from which the bread was distributed. He closed the door and went to the church, and the brothers saw his face shining brightly, and they were amazed. **141.** When they left the church, [our father] went to his dwelling, and when it was time, they were summoned so that each one should come to his work. The brother who was in charge of the bread-store came to the old man and said: 'My holy father, of your charity, come and pray so that we can open another bread-store and bring out what we need for those who come to us. There is little left[89] in the one from which we are bringing it [at the moment]'. The old man's face filled with joy and he said: 'Go, my son, bring out [all] that is there until there is none left'. The brother said to him: 'Forgive me, my father, I left nothing in that bread-store save one basket which I would like you to bless'. The old man said to him: 'Arise, and bring out the basket which you left

---

*Ps 116:12

behind'. **142.** When the steward[90] went to open the door
of the bread-store, he could not open it, and when the
brothers got up and pushed it, they could not open it either.
'Clearly', they said, 'it is not God's will that we should
provide for the multitudes today'. Our father apa Shenoute
knew what had happened and he arose, went to the brothers,
and said to them: 'Arise and bring forth the Lord's abundance, and if it should not be enough, we will open another
[store-room] and draw from that'. When they had prayed,
the old man made the sign [of the cross] on the door, saying: 'My Lord God, by your power and your command, let
the door be opened!'. **143.** The door then opened immediately, and from inside a great heap of bread poured forth,
and there was such a mass of bread that it filled up the door-
way. In this way, the multitudes and the brothers were sup-
plied for six months by the abundance of bread which came
forth from the door of the bread-store, and to this very day
that bread-store is called 'the Store-Room of the Blessing'.

**144.** There was a brother-monk [who used to work] in
the brother's vegetable garden whose name was Psoti, and he
was exceedingly charitable. He would give vegetables to every
man who came to him, especially to the brothers [dwelling]
on the mountain. **145.** The brothers accused him of his
excessive generosity before our father apa Shenoute, saying:
'Psoti will leave nothing in the brothers' vegetable garden,
and neither we nor those who come to us will find what we
need'. Our father, in the love of God, said to them: 'If you
have not run out of vegetables, he is guilty of no sin. Nevertheless, we will go to him at daybreak and rebuke him, and if
we are in need, we will remove him from the garden. Yet what
a great thing is charity!'. For my father apa Shenoute knew
that [Psoti] was blessed in everything he did. **146.** Now
that night, when the old man had finished praying and lay
down for a little while, he saw in a trance a very beautiful
woman whose whole body shone with light like the sun. She
took the hand of Psoti and spoke with him, saying: 'See

that you do not stop your charity in the vegetable garden.
Do you own the earth which gives its fruit? Do you own the
water in the cistern? Do you own the strength of the beasts
who labour? Behold, I say to you, the heart of my Lord
and my Son is satisfied with you because you give a few
vegetables to the brothers and all who are in need'.
**147.** When our holy father apa Shenoute heard these words
which the woman said to Psoti the gardener, he knew that
she was the Mother of the Lord. She then turned to the old
man apa Shenoute and said: 'Shenoute, beloved of my son,
behold! I bring to you him whom they accused before you.
If you find in him any sin, I will punish him with a serious
illness'. **148.** When the old man the prophet awoke from
the vision, he was amazed at what had happened; and when
they were summoned to the church, the old man went into
the church before the brothers went in and saw Psoti the
gardener standing in prayer with his ten fingers burning and
shining like flaming lamps. Our father said to him: 'Who are
you [whom I see] like this?'. He said to him: 'I am Psoti,
your son'. The old man said to him: 'Who brought you here,
my son?'. Psoti said to him: 'He who came to you in your
room and spoke with you before [the brothers] were
summoned to the church, it was he who brought me here'.
The old man said to him: 'My son, it is written: "Your God
is God, and the Lord of Lords is your king"*. Behold!
I know that God is with you in all that you do. Today I will
come to you in the garden to visit you, but for your part, my
son, give alms just as you have done'. **149.** Then, at the
third hour of the day, the old man went to him secretly in the
garden and saw Psoti gathering vegetables for the brothers.
Apa Psoti arose and received our father's blessing, saying: 'A
great blessing has come upon me today, my holy father, because you have come to me: we will be blessed in all

---

*Cf. Rv 17:14*

that we do'. **150.** The holy old man apa Shenoute then saw the holy Virgin Mary with a bowl of water placed before her. She guided the hands of apa Psoti to [the bowl], sprinkled the water over all the vegetables, and spoke thus: 'Grow, and never stop'. After that, she gave him peace and departed from him in great glory. Then our father apa Shenoute knew that the holy apa Psoti was exceptionally righteous and that the Lord Jesus was with him in everything he did.

**151.** Another day, when our father apa Shenoute was sitting talking with some laymen, a raven settled on the wall above them and croaked down at them. Then one of the men sitting by our father looked up at the raven and said: 'Is that good news in your beak, raven?' **152.** Our father apa Shenoute sighed and said: 'What foolishness prevails among the sons of men! How can this raven know this good news? Is the raven your father's messenger? No, my son; do not again put it in your heart to listen to this bird. He is only calling to the Lord to get his dinner ready! Have you not heard David the psalmist saying, "It is he who gives their food to the beasts and to the young ravens who call out to him"*. **153.** For there are many men who take auguries from the voice of birds, and from the sun, moon, or stars. All these things are idolatrous and evil, for it is written, "As for the man that does these things, I will obliterate that man from among his people"†. Again, there are many who put their trust in the princes of this world so that no evil will befall them. They themselves do not know that if God turned his face from them,** they could not stand for a single hour, for it is written, "Do not put your trust in princes or in the sons of men, for when their spirit goes from them and they return to the earth, on that day all their thoughts shall perish. Happy is he whose helper is the God of Jacob, and

---

*Ps 147:9
†Lv 20:6
**Cf. Ps 13:1 and elsewhere

whose hope is fixed on the Lord his God" '*.

**154.** Once, when our father apa Shenoute went into the desert, behold! the Lord Jesus appeared to him and spoke with him. As they were walking together, they came upon a corpse cast out upon the mountain.[91] Our father apa Shenoute threw himself down and worshipped the Lord, and said to him: 'My Lord and my God, behold, for many years I have passed by this corpse without knowing why it was destined to be cast out here'. **155.** Our Lord Jesus Christ touched the corpse with his foot and said to it: 'Corpse, I say to you, recover yourself and rise up so that you can tell my servant Shenoute who you are, [cast out] like this'. The corpse immediately arose, just as someone would arise from sleep, and when it saw the Lord, it recognised him and worshipped him, and said to him: 'My Lord, let your mercy come upon me!' The Saviour said to him: 'Speak, and let my chosen one, Shenoute, know what you have done'. The corpse said: 'What shall I say, my Lord? You know what is hidden and what is revealed, and you know what was my fate'. The Saviour said to it: 'Nevertheless, speak, so that my servant Shenoute may hear you himself'. **156.** The corpse replied: 'I am a glassblower from Siōout who was working with some other men. We arose and went south near to Šmin so that we could work there, but after a few days had passed, I became ill and died. So because none of them was related to me by blood, they brought me here and cast me forth'. **157.** My father apa Shenoute said to him: 'Had the Saviour come into the world at that time?' He said: 'Yes, he had. The news had been spread abroad and came south to us by those passing through [the area] that a woman had entered the city of Šmoun[92] with a little boy in her arms. Everything he said came to pass: he would raise the dead, he would cast out demons, he would make the lame walk, he would make the deaf hear, he would make the dumb speak, he would cleanse

*Ps 146:3-5

lepers;* in a word, he was performing every [possible] sign.
When I heard these things, I resolved in my heart to go
north[93] to worship him, but [worldly] cares did not permit
it.' **158.** When the corpse had said these things, it prostrated
itself and worshipped the Saviour and asked him: 'Let your
mercy come upon me, and do not let me be cast into
torments again. Woe is me, that the womb of my mother was
not my tomb before I descended to these sufferings!'
**159.** The Lord said to him: 'Inasmuch as you have been
worthy to see me on earth, together with my servant apa
Shenoute, I will give you a little relief. Lie down now so that
mercy may come upon you, and rest until the day of the true
judgement'. Straightaway the corpse lay down just as it was
at first. **160.** The Saviour took the hand of our father apa
Shenoute and walked with him to the cell in the desert, and
they spoke of great mysteries between them. After this,
[the Lord] ascended into the heavens with angels singing
before him.

**161.** After these things, some men brought to [my
father] a camel who had given birth. Her foal, which was
following her, was very feeble because [the mother] would
never let it take suck of her breast. When our father saw
her, he brought a little water from the basin in the church
and gave it to her, and she drank it. He then put her son
under her and said: 'If you will not accept your son, why
did you ever give him birth?' Straightaway, she gave him
milk without any trouble. After this, her owners took her
and returned to their home glorifying God and our holy
father apa Shenoute.

**162.** There was a man in the nome of Šmin, a hired work-
man, who worked for his wages on a yearly [contract], and
whose sons did not have enough bread. He arose, went to our
father the prophet apa Shenoute, and began to entreat him
[for help], but my father knew immediately why he had

---

*Mt 11:5; Lk 7:22

come to him. **163.** Then the man said to him: 'My holy father, let your mercy come upon me! I have worked since my childhood, working for this man and that, and after all this I and my sons do not have enough bread; instead, we are in want from day to day'. Our father said to him: 'My son, perhaps you have not found the sort of work by which you can make a living'. And [the man] said to him: 'I do not know, my holy father'. **164.** Our father went into the church and prayed, and entreated the Lord on his behalf, and when he had finished praying, he found a few gourd seeds. These he took, dipped them in the water on the altar, and gave them to the man, saying: 'Take these few gourd-seeds, go along a certain road and there plant yourself a gourd. It is this work which the Lord has ordained for you so that you can make a living. But if [the gourd] grows well, I have a share in it; it is destined for me as well as you. The man replied: 'Most certainly, my holy father!'. **165.** The man went and planted the gourd, and then came back again, went to our father and said to him: 'Behold, I planted the gourd, but pray for me so that I may go and work twenty more days to complete the full year in the place where I work'. **166.** After this, he went and worked at the gourd, and when it had grown, he gathered the first-fruits and took them to the monastery. Our father took them and distributed them to the brothers. Then he prayed over a little water and gave it to [the man], saying: 'Sprinkle this small amount of water over it and say to it: "Shenoute said: Grow tall, for I have a share in you".' The man took the water, sprinkled it over the gourd and said to it: 'The holy apa Shenoute said: "Grow tall, for I have a share in you".'

**167.** The gourd began to spread out and develop, bringing forth beautiful fruit, and it multiplied greatly. Then the poor man began to sell, and acquired a mass of wheat, barley, lentils, bread, and all sorts of things, and the poor man became very rich. He filled his house with all good things so that he needed others to work at gathering in the fruit of the

gourd because there was so much of it.⁹⁴ When he had a sur-
feit of all good things, the gourd died.⁹⁵  **168.** The man
arose and went to the monastery prostrated himself before
my father and said: 'My holy father, because of your holy
prayers, God has favoured me with a great quantity of good
things. Arise now, let us go and divide between us the Lord's
bounty'. Our father arose and followed him in his great sim-
plicity with his palm-branch in his hand. When he came to the
man's house, he saw the granaries [full] of bread and wheat,
[**169.**] and the old man tested him to see his temptation
and his intention. The man said to him: 'Divide the Lord's
bounty between us. See, I have prepared the carts and the
camels so that they can take your share to the monastery'.
When my father saw the nature of his faith and his intention,
he said to him: 'My son, Shenoute wants nothing; instead,
take all these things for yourself and live off them with your
sons. I trust in God that from this day you will never again
lack any good thing; instead, be charitable yourself. But
arise, let us go so that you can show me the gourd'.  **170.**  So
when they had come to the place where the gourd was, they
saw that it had died. Our father touched it with the palm-
branch he had in his hand and said to it: 'Gourd, I say to you,
grow, and produce a little more fruit for this poor man so
that he and his sons can live'. Thus our holy father apa
Shenoute returned to the monastery, and afterwards the
gourd flourished again and produced beautiful fruit.
**171.** The man became exceedingly rich, and the bounty
which the Lord had ordained for him the first time he
ordained for him a second time in the same way. Thereafter,
he bought and sold in gold and fruit, and acquired great
quantities of goods and piles of riches which neither his
parents nor his parents' parents had ever seen. He therefore
glorified God and our father the prophet apa Shenoute all
the days of his life until he died.
    **172.**   Behold, then, we have told you just a small selec-
tion of the marvels and ascetic practices of our father the

holy prophet apa Shenoute, the apostle and celibate, the priest and archimandrite, which I, Besa, the disciple of my father the old man, saw with my eyes and heard with my ears. He was exalted in his generation as high as the palm-tree and his fruit multiplied like the cedar-wood of Lebanon,* so that his good renown spread abroad and filled the face of the whole earth like the plants of the earth. He triumphed victoriously over all the power of the enemy because of the profusion of his blessed tears, the stability of his angelic life, and the establishment of his holy community, which was still renowned after his death.

**173.** But let us return again to his good progress so that we may obtain his grace. With his discourse and his letters, holy and seasoned with salt,† our father apa Shenoute would instruct everyone, both small and great,[96] monk or layman. He would command them to be hospitable and merciful to one and all, especially so that charity, peace, and righteousness should abide in the monastery at all times.

**174.** Our father was [now] very old and filled with good days like our fathers the patriarchs. Many times our righteous father proclaimed to all of us these words: 'The Lord has favoured me with the lifespan of Moses the archprophet: one hundred and twenty years. But if you anger me, I shall pray that he take me away before those years [are accomplished]'. **175.** When our father apa Shenoute was advanced in days and was nearly one hundred and eighteen years old, he began to be ill on the first day of the month Epiphi[97]. This, as he told us, was the day on which he was born. **176.** He then said to me, Besa, his disciple: 'I would like a few boiled vegetables'. I went quickly to the place where the visiting brothers eat and took him some to eat. He said to me: 'Take it and put it on the roof until I ask for it', and I did what he said. **177.** On the third day of his illness he said to me: 'Go and bring me those few boiled [vegetables]'. I brought

*Cf. Ps 92:12
†Cf. Col 4:6

them to him, but when he opened his mouth, he found that they were stinking like a cast-out corpse. He said to himself: 'Soul, you wanted this; eat it!'. But afterwards he said to me: 'Take it and throw it away'. So he did not taste it.

**178.** Then from that day, the sickness weighed down on him [more and more] until the sixth day came, the sixth day of Epiphi[98], and he had the senior brothers of the monastery called in to him and spoke to us like this: 'My beloved sons, I have asked for you all [to come here] because truly it is my Lord's will that he take me from this temporary dwelling and separate my soul from my miserable body'. **179.** I, together with the brothers who were round him, threw myself down upon him, and we wept greatly and said to him: 'Our father, will you go and leave us orphans? Where will we find a man like you to teach us and fill us with both kinds of food, the divine and the human? You have filled the whole world with your holy precepts and your words of wisdom with which God favoured you; your words and your rules, your ordinances and your apostolic commands have filled the whole world'. **180.** He said to us again: 'Keep my commandments which I enjoined upon you. See that you do not neglect the ordinances which I taught you from the Lord: brotherly love, mercy, hospitality to the needy and to strangers. Do not let these come to an end in the holy monasteries; accept them one and all for the love of Christ, so that the angels of God may also come to you and dwell with you. Do not neglect the worship, prayers, and fasts, but persevere[99] in them at all times so that you may be companions of Christ, and by keeping these things you will not lack any good thing, either here or in the world to come'. **181.** His illness was again getting worse, and we were all weeping for him and grieved at heart.

**182.** When morning came on the seventh day of this month Epiphi[100], he was in great pain from his illness. At the sixth hour of the day, I said to him: 'My father, how are you now?' He said to me: 'Woe is me, for the road is long. How long must I wait before I go to God? There are terrors and strong powers upon the path; woe is me until I meet the Lord'. **183.** When he had said these things, he was silent and in a coma for half an hour. Suddenly he cried out: 'Of your charity, my holy fathers, bless me; come and sit before me in your ordered ranks.[101] **184.** He said again: 'Behold! the patriarchs have come with the prophets; behold the apostles with the archbishops; behold the archimandrites have come with all the saints'. **185.** Again he said: 'My father apa Pšoi,[103] my father apa Antony,[103] my father apa Pachomius,[104] take my hand so that I may rise and worship him whom my soul loves, for behold! he has come for me with his angels!' **186.** At that moment, there came a great fragrance. Then, on that day, the seventh of Epiphi, he gave his soul into the hands of God.

**187.** And behold! there came sounds in the monastery. We heard sweet voices crying out over his holy body and uttering hymns and psalms and spiritual songs,* choir by choir. **188.** This is what they were saying: 'Peace be with you, O Shenoute, and at your meeting with God. Today the heavens will rejoice with you, O you who would not permit the devil to appear in any of your monasteries. Peace be with you, O Shenoute, friend of God and beloved of Christ, brother of all the saints. We all rejoice with you, you who brought edification to perfection and kept the faith, who have received a shining crown.† Behold! the gates of heaven have opened for you that rejoicing you may go in through them!'.

**189.** When we had heard these things, we quickly covered his holy body, laid it in an inlaid [?] chest,[105] and buried him.[106] We sat weeping and grieved at heart for him, for we had lost a great and good teacher. **190.** In this way, we again glorified God and offered thanks to our Lord and our God, our king, our Saviour, Jesus Christ, to whom be glory with his good Father and the holy and life-giving

*Cf. Eph 5:19, Col 3:16
†Cf. 2 Tm 4:7-8

Spirit now and for ever and unto the ages of all ages.
Amen.

NOTES

*Abbreviations*

[B]  Bohairic Coptic
[S]  Sahidic Coptic
[G]  Greek
[L]  Latin

1. The idea that ascetic practices could produce miraculous powers was fairly common in Egypt, and is a concept shared by a number of cultures. It is not difficult to find examples of these early ascetics 'prophesying', and Shenoute is not especially unusual in this regard. John of Lycopolis (see n. 79 below) was a noted prophet, though according to Palladius it took him thirty years of solitary asceticism to be deemed worthy of the gift (see *Palladius: The Lausiac History,* tr. R. T. Meyer [Westminster, 1965] 99 [ = XXXV, 2]), and in 345 c.e., the great Pachomius was arraigned before a synod of bishops in Latopolis (the modern Esna, midway between Luxor and Edfu) on charges relating to his clairvoyance (see *Pachomian Koinonia* I, tr. A. Veilleux [CS 45; Kalamazoo, 1980] 375-377 [ = *Vita Prima Graeca* 112]). It should be noted, however, that the term 'prophet' did not always signify someone who could produce oracles: it could also refer simply to a wonder-worker or charismatic (see H. E. Winlock and W. E. Crum, *The Monastery of Epiphanius at Thebes* [New York, 1926; rpt. 1973] 1:213 n. 10).
2. *Apa* [SB] is a title of reverence corresponding to the more formal Greek *abba.* Both derive from the Syriac *abba* 'father'. H. I. Bell seems to have assumed that the term referred only to ordained priests (see his *Jews and Christians in Egypt* [London, 1924] 43, 45), but this is not correct. *Abba* rather than *apa* is used of Shenoute in the passage from the *Life of Pijimi* translated in n. 91 below.
3. 7th Epiphi (*epep* [S]; *epēp* [B])=1st July. On the Coptic calendar,

93

see De Lacy O'Leary, *The Saints of Egypt* (London, 1937; rpt. Amsterdam, 1974) 34-35, and O.F.A. Meinardus, *Christian Egypt: Ancient and Modern* (Cairo, 1972²) 70-74. There is also a *mûlid* of Shenoute held at the White Monastery two weeks after this on 14th July (see *ibid.* 156, and *ibid.* 138-144 for a discussion of the nature and importance of these *mawâlid*).

4. 'Old man' (*hello* [S] ; *chellō* [B] ) is here a technical term and, as Armand Veilleux points out, refers to one's experience in the monastic life rather than one's age (*Pachomian Koinonia I* 272, 275). An 'old man', in other words, is a spiritual father and guide.

5. *Lit.* 'sea of waters'.

6. *Polētia/poletia* is the Coptic form of the Greek *politeia* which is a word of wide meaning. It may signify citizenship, polity, commonwealth, state, civil affairs, a way of life, or ascetic practices (see G. W. H. Lampe, *A Patristic Greek Lexicon* [Oxford, 1961] s.v.). It is this last meaning which applies here: 'the ascetic way of life proper to a monk' (*Pachomian Koinonia I* 269).

7. Amélineau has identified Šenalolet with the modern village of Shandawîl, situated on the west bank of the Nile and less than a dozen miles from both Akhmîm (see n. 9 below) and the White Monastery (see E. Amélineau, *La géographie de l'Égypte à l'époque Copte* [Paris, 1893] 426-428).

8. In Coptic *toš* [S] ; *thoš/thōš* [B] originally referred to a 'nome' (Late Egyptian *tš*), one of the administrative districts into which Egypt had been divided since early times. In Christian Egypt, however, the same term was used for a bishopric or diocese, the boundaries of which often, but not always, corresponded to those of the nome. In this present translation, for the sake of consistency, I have rendered the term by 'nome' throughout.

9. The Coptic Šmin is the Greek Panopolis and the modern Akhmîm, and it lies about three hundred miles up the Nile from Cairo. It was a thriving nome-capital in its day, and in the Christian period was the centre of a large number of monasteries. The White Monastery is about seven miles distant on the opposite bank of the river. See further Amélineau, *Géographie* 18-22.

10. Tybi (*tōbe* [S]; *tōbi* [B] ) is the fifth month of the Egyptian calendar and lasts from 27th December to 25th January.

11. Apa Pjol was Shenoute's uncle on his mother's side (see *Vita* 7), and it was he who, in the middle of the fourth century, founded the White Monastery. His own temperament was eremitic rather

than coenobitic, and although he based his own rule on that of Pachomius, he made it more severe and rigorous. Pachomius, for example, permitted his monks to eat bread twice a day, but Pjol seems to have reduced this to once. Partly, perhaps, as a consequence of this fierce asceticism, Pjol's community was never large—there were less than thirty brothers at the time of his death—and the real fame of the White Monastery dates from the time of Shenoute, who succeeded his uncle as abbot in about 385 (see Introduction nn. 46-47). Pjol is not commemorated in the *Synaxarium*, though he was remembered at the White Monastery itself, where his feast was celebrated on 29th Mechir (*mšir* [S]; *mechir* [B]) = 23rd February. For further discussion, see J. Leipoldt, *Schenute von Atripe und die Entstehung des national ägyptischen Christentums* (Leipzig, 1903) 36-39 and his index s.v. Pgōl. Little can be added to this account, for the sources on Pjol are very meagre, and no *Vita* is recorded.

12. This is a loose translation to bring out the sense. *Archōn* [GSB] may mean 'ruler', as I have rendered it here (i.e. the leading members of the local civil administration), or more specifically 'magistrates (*magistratus* [L]: see H. J. Mason, *Greek Terms for Roman Institutions: A Lexicon and Analysis* [Toronto, 1974] 110-113). The translation 'prince' (*princeps* [L]) which appears fairly frequently accords with this second usage, for as Mason points out: 'the use of *archōn* for *princeps* follows naturally both from its common use in Greek for the first official of a city, and from its application to various Roman magistrates. The *princeps* viewed as the first magistrate is consistent with the usage of the Latin word' (*ibid.* 112).

13. *Keleli* [B]: the sonorous wooden board which is beaten with a wooden hammer to summon the brethren in many orthodox monasteries. They vary in size, but the larger and longer ones would make a formidable weapon. According to Leipoldt, however, the practice in the White Monastery was to use a metal plate rather than a wooden board (see his *Schenute* 131).

14. Little is known of apa Pšoi of Mount Psōou, and he must be distinguished from the much more famous Pšoi who was one of the early settlers in Scetis and the great friend of Paul of Tamwah (see n. 102 below). Crum, following the *Synaxarium*, relates his life as follows: 'A native of Achmîm, his life in youth was evil, till, falling ill, he had a vision of hell, where he beheld thieves . . . cut in four by angels. In terror he vows to repent and, if God heal him, never again to behold a woman. Recovering, he goes to the

monastery of Banwaît, is received by the monks, and there for
many years fights the spiritual fight, till his fame is spread
abroad and he is made head 'over many saints'. He composed
many admonitions and instructions for monks and laity, and,
after thirty-five years of rigorous asceticism, died' (W. E.
Crum, 'A Study in the History of Egyptian Monasticism' in *Journal of
Theological Studies* OS 5 [1904] 132). According to tradition,
he was the founder of the Red Monastery on Mount Psōou, which
lies about four miles from the White Monastery of Pjol and
about a dozen miles from the monastery at Banwaît mentioned
in the entry in the *Synaxarium*. Pšoi is commemorated on
5th Mechir = 30th January. See further, Leipoldt, *Schenute*
36-37. For a description of the Red Monastery, see A. J. Butler,
*The Ancient Coptic Churches of Egypt* (Oxford, 1884; rpt. 1970)
1:357-359; Meinardus, *Christian Egypt: Ancient and Modern*
404-406; and C. C. Walters, *Monastic Archaeology in Egypt*
(Warminster, 1974) Index s.v. 'Deir el Ahmar'. Both Meinardus
and Walters provide further bibliographies. There is a photograph
of the interior in J. G. Milne, *A History of Egypt Under Roman
Rule* (London, 1924³) 96.

15.  *Lit.* 'say'.

16.  *Poletia* [SB] / *politeia* [G]: see n. 6. above.

17.  Psoi was the Egyptian name for the city of Ptolemaïs Hermiou,
founded by Ptolemy I Soter I (323-285 b.c.e.). Its modern name
is El-Manshâh/Minshâh/Menshîya, and it lies about eight miles up
river from Akhmîm. It was described by Strabo as 'the largest of
the cities in the Thebaid and no smaller than Memphis, with a
form of government modelled on that of the Greeks' (Strabo,
*Geography* XVII, i, 42). Over the centuries, however, its fortunes
declined, and the 1929 Baedeker described it simply as 'a dirty
town of fellahîn' (K. Baedeker, *Egypt and the Sûdân: Handbook
for Travellers* [Leipzig/London, 1929⁸] 230). See further
Amélineau, *Géographie* 381-383. According to the latter, the
village of Psenkhōout corresponds to the modern village of
Samhûd, about thirty miles south of El-Manshâh (see his
*Géographie* 412-413).

18.  *Thermēsi* [B] = *tremis* [L]. Under the later Roman emperors, a
*tremis* was the third part of an *aureus,* and an *aureus* was the
standard gold coin of Rome. It was actually a reasonable amount
of money, but certainly not enough to sustain one in a life of
luxury. One *tremis* would buy 3½ *artabas* of corn (see W. E.
Crum, *Coptic Ostraca from the Collections of the Egypt*

*Exploration Fund, the Cairo Museum and Others* [London, 1902] #257: in Egypt at this time, one *artaba* was about 6.66 gallons or 30 litres), or twelve suits of clothes (*lit.* 'twelve pairs [*soeish* (S)] of linen garments': see *ibid.* #Ad. 30). It was also equivalent to 9½ 'baskets' of bronze money (see *ibid.* #174: the 'basket' [*liknon* (G)] seems to have indicated a large number of coins of low denomination [*ibid.* #48 n. 3]).

19. *Doux* [GSB] = *dux* [L]. A 'duke' was a military commander-in-chief, and his area of jurisdiction could cover a province, part of a province, or even several provinces, depending on time and place. At one stage, the whole of Egypt and Libya was under the military administration of a single *dux* (the *dux Aegypti Thebaidis utrarumque Libyarum*), but in Shenoute's time this was no longer the case. By the end of the reign of Theodosius I (see n. 53 below) the army in Egypt was commanded by a *comes rei militaris* or *comes Aegypti* (see n. 88 below) under whom were two *duces:* the *dux Thebaidis* stationed in Antinoë/Antinoupolis (see n. 51 below), who is referred to here, and the *dux Libyarum.* We might also note that in Egypt the old Roman policy of keeping the civil and military administration strictly separate was not always adhered to, and by the fifth century the *dux Thebaidis* wielded civil as well as military powers in Upper Egypt. For further discussion of the titles, natures, and functions of the *duces,* see A. H. M. Jones, *The Later Roman Empire 284–602* (Oxford, 1964) Index s.v. '*dux*'.

20. This is a loose translation to bring out the sense; the Coptic, Arabic, and Syriac versions differ as to the whereabouts of the duke. According to the Arabic *Life,* he was to be found on a boat in the river; according to the Syriac version published by Nau (see Introduction n. 31), he and his attendants were at the gate of the city of Šmin.

21. Cyril of Alexandria, who became patriarch of Alexandria in 412 and who was primarily responsible for the condemnation and excommunication of Nestorius (see the Introduction to this study, and n. 23 below). His character, and his role in the complicated Christological controversy are discussed in all the standard textbooks, and we need not dwell upon them here. Cyril died in 444 on 3rd Epiphi = 27th June, and is commemorated on that day in the Coptic *Synaxarium* (see O'Leary, *Saints of Egypt* 116-118).

22. Apa Victor is Victor of Tabennesi, the first community founded by Pachomius in about 320 c.e. (see n. 104 below). It is the modern Nag'-el-Sabrîyât, lying midway between Fâw and Dechna,

and some seventy miles up the river from Akhmîm. According to O'Leary, apa Victor attended the council of Constantinople in 381, together with Shenoute, but that was some considerable time before the events narrated here. The Nestorian controversy did not begin until about 428, and if the meeting between Cyril, Victor, and Shenoute referred to here is, in fact, historical, then it probably took place in 430 c.e. Victor seems to have been present at the council of Ephesus, again with Shenoute, in 431 (see n. 85 below), and to have died sometime between that council and the great council of Chalcedon in 451. Leipoldt (*Schenute* 159) puts his death at ± 440. See further O'Leary, *Saints of Egypt* 281.

23. Nestorius, a zealous and devout Antiochene, was elevated to the see of Constantinople in 428, and when his chaplain, Anastasius, preached against the use of the title *Theotokos,* 'God-bearer', in referring to Mary, Nestorius gave him his support and thereby lit the fuse that was to explode in the great Christological contro- versy. Nestorius was accused (unjustly) of refusing to use the title *Theotokos,* and of implying as a consequence that Jesus was not God. Instead (said his enemies), he taught that Jesus was no more than an ordinary human being who became the Son of God when the Holy Spirit descended on him at his baptism. In fact, there is not the slightest doubt that Nestorius, though not without fault, was both misunderstood and deliberately mis- represented, and the picture of him which emerges from Besa's *Life* is certainly biased. His protestations of innocence, however, went unheard, and he and his alleged teachings were condemned at the council of Ephesus in 431 and again at Chalcedon in 451. See further J. F. Bethune-Baker, *Nestorius and His Teaching* (Cambridge, 1908) and F. Loofs, *Nestorius and His Place in the History of Christian Doctrine* (Cambridge, 1914), and the excel- lent and indispensable study of Luigi I. Scipioni, *Nestorio e il concilio di Efeso. Storia, dogma, critica; Studia Patristica Mediolanensia I* (Milan, 1974). There are important critical reviews of this last work by C. Kannengiesser in *Revue d'histoire ecclésiastique* 73 (1978) 669-672, and by G. Jouassard, in *ibid.* 74 (1979) 346-348 ('Le cas de Nestorius').

24. Constantinople. So too in *Vita* 56 ff.

25. *Smou* [SB] in Coptic means both 'blessing' and 'abundance', and usually implies both. You cannot have the latter without the former.

26. *Lit.* 'turn it back' (*kōl ebol* [B]: see W. E. Crum, *A Coptic*

*Dictionary* [Oxford, 1939; rpt. 1979] 807a).

27. There were two occasions for communal worship (*synaxis*) each day at the White Monastery: one in the morning before the day's work began and one in the evening after the communal meal. Each *synaxis* followed the same pattern: there were a number of readings of scriptural passages (twelve such readings seems to have been the standard number), and each reading was followed by a short prayer. On Saturdays and Sundays the *synaxis* ,seems to have been lengthened to include a sermon, and on Sunday at least, there was a celebration of the Eucharist (see n. 71 below). For further details, see Leipoldt, *Schenute* 129-130. In this present translation I have rendered *synaxis* by 'worship' throughout.

28. *Lakh* [SB] can mean 'corner, extremity, top, angle, piece, or fragment' (Crum, *Dictionary* 140b). The Syriac version of Nau has Shenoute 'sitting on a rock at the gate of his monastery'.

29. *Lit.* 'because you are a little son' (*oukouji nšēri* [B] ). 'Little sons' is a standard expression in Coptic for the novices or newcomers to a monastery. The senior brothers are then referred to as the 'great sons' (see n. 77 below).

30. *Lit.* 'No, but you are small in heart'. 'Faint-hearted' would be the usual translation for 'small in heart' (*kouji nhēt* [B]), and as such it is rendered in Wiesmann's Latin translation of Besa's *Life* (see the bibliography at the end of this volume; the term is *pusillus*). It may also be defended, as Kuhn defends it, by what we know from other sources of Besa's character (see K. H. Kuhn, 'A Fifth-Century Egyptian Abbot' in *Journal of Theological Studies* 5 [1954] 46-47). Crum, however, also suggests 'impatient' (see *Dictionary* 93b and 714b), and this too could well fit the circumstances: Besa is still young and has achieved neither the sanctity nor the experience which would enable him to see Christ in the flesh. Amélineau, in the French translation which accompanies his edition of the Bohairic *Life* (p. 17) simply translates the phrase literally: 'tu es petit de coeur' (see also his *Les moines égyptiens: Vie de Schnoudi* [Paris, 1889] 118). Personally, I would prefer to read it as 'impatient'.

31. The Syriac version published by Nau adds the further clarification: '. . . I was grateful to him for his great goodness to me, but I was not worthy to see him corporeally'.

32. See n. 17 above.

33. For 'I trust (*tinhti* [B]) in God . . . ' Amélineau suggested the emendation 'Trust (*nahti* [B]) in God . . . ' , and this reading is

confirmed by one of the fragments of the *Life of Shenoute*
which came from the monastery of St Macarius in Scetis (see
H. G. Evelyn White, *The Monasteries of the Wadi'n-Natrûn*
[New York, 1926; rpt. 1973] 1:163.

34. Illustrations and descriptions of the type of ovens used in the
Egyptian monasteries may be found in Winlock/Crum, *Monastery
of Epiphanius* 53-54, and Walters, *Monastic Archaeology* 207-
209. Baking was certainly not a daily occurrence: at the White
Monastery it may well have been done only twice a year (*ibid.*
162, 171), and at Tabennesi there was a single annual baking (see
the Bohairic *Life* of Pachomius 77 [*Pachomian Koinonia* I:100]).
To understand this, we must remember that the bread was very
hard and dry like ship's biscuit, and had to be soaked before it
could be eaten.

35. What exactly did Shenoute find? The Coptic has *askalōnē,* and
although it is obvious that this is Greek, it is not so obvious what
it means. In a footnote to his French translation (p. 20 n. 4),
Amélineau admits the word is unknown to him, but goes on to
say that it undoubtedly refers to 'an earthenware flask coming
perhaps from Ascalon'. *Askalōnē,* however, is not to be found in
any of the standard classical dictionaries, and if Amélineau is
not correct, one might suggest instead that the word is related in
some way to *askos* [G], which means a leather bag (usually, but
not necessarily, a wine-skin), but this suggestion, too, involves
certain linguistic difficulties. Whatever it was, it was something
which could be 'spent' or 'sold' (*jko* [B]) to build a church, and
I have therefore suggested 'bag [of gold]'. This certainly fits the
context, but whether it is quite correct is another matter.

36. Pemje is the Egyptian name of the ancient Oxyrhynchus and was
once the capital of a nome. In the early christian period it
attracted multitudes of monks, and the town was as full of
churches as the surrounding countryside was of monasteries.
Under Islam, its fortunes gradually began to decline, and according to the invaluable Baedeker, this once populous city is now
represented 'only by a few desolate heaps of débris' (Baedeker,
*Egypt and the Sûdân* 219). Its modern name is El-Banasâ/
Behnesa, and it is a considerable distance down-river from
Akhmîm. See further, Amélineau, *Géographie* 90-93.

37. The term 'great man' (*ništi nrōmi* [B]) is not just a flattering
description, but a semi-official title. It was applied to civil as
well as to ecclesiastical dignitaries, but here (and elsewhere in
similar literature) it is equivalent to archimandrite. See further

Winlock/Crum, *Monastery of Epiphanius* 1:131 and Crum, *Coptic Ostraca* 53 #119 n. 2.

38. *Lit.* 'the hair of his head'. This is a standard expression and occurs elsewhere (see, for example, *Vita* 42). The purpose of the combing was cleanliness, not beautification (see further Amélineau, *Vie de Schnoudi* 170 n. 1).

39. The location of Komentios is unknown to us. Amélineau (*Géographie* 229) offers no identification, and the encyclopedic *Dizionario dei nomi geografici e topografici dell'Egitto Greco-Romano* of Aristide Calderini (Cairo/Madrid/Milan, 1935–) has not yet reached the letter K. The name does not appear to be Coptic, but what it means and where it was remain obscure. According to Besa, the man came from 'the country outside [the borders of Egypt]', and the Arabic *Life* is of no more help: we are simply told that he came from 'a distant village'.

40. *Sioout,* the Greek Lycopolis, is the modern Asyût. It lies about sixty miles downriver from Akhmîm and is the largest town in Upper Egypt.

41. Besa, of course, gives the Coptic name of Alexandria: *Rakoti* [B] / *Rakote* [S].

42. One of the fragments of Shenoute's *Life* from the monastery of St Macarius (see n. 33 above) adds an additional sentence here: 'Then the man said: "I entreat you, O my holy father, . . . pray for me so that the Lord may direct my path in peace". And after[?] he had received a blessing, he went away' (see Evelyn White, *Monasteries of the Wadi'n-Natrûn* 1:163).

43. Amélineau has identified Chereu with the tiny village of El-Kerîoun lying some twenty-four miles south-east of Alexandria. In Shenoute's time it was of much greater consequence, and was the last place a traveller would have rested overnight before entering Alexandria the next day (see Amélineau, *Géographie* 217-218).

44. *Lit.* 'table for taking the sacrament' (*trapeza nǧismou* [B]). Crum's suggestion of 'portative altar' (see his *Dictionary* 337b) is probably correct.

45. The sense of this sentence is not entirely clear, although the Coptic is not difficult to translate. It seems to me that two points are involved: (i) the businessman has already lost some of his possessions through no fault of his own: first of all he was robbed, and then, after he had had his goods returned to him, Shenoute made him give some of them to the robber; (ii) now, because of his debt to Shenoute, he knows that he could never

take any money from him for the altar, and whatever he spent on it would therefore be lost. In other words, he would be throwing away his own money with his own hands, and that is something he is not prepared to do. It is clear from Shenoute's comments in *Vita* 52 that the businessman has far too great an interest in the riches of this world, and fails to realize that they are something which is here today and gone tomorrow.

46. *Lit.* 'a month of days'. This is a standard expression and occurs elsewhere (see, for example, n. 76 below).

47. *Lit.* 'lays her hand with another'. The expression means 'to make an agreement/contract' (Crum, *Dictionary* 338a).

48. *Eusebēs* [G] / *pius* [L], 'pious', was on occasion used as an imperial title, the most obvious example being Antoninus Pius, Roman emperor from 137 to 161. Lampe (*Patristic Greek Lexicon* 576 s.v. *eusebēs* 6) gives further examples of the term being applied to Constantine, Licinius, Constantius, Honorius, and deceased emperors in general. See also *Vita* 76 for the same term.

49. Theodosius II (401-450) was Eastern Roman Emperor from 408, but his great personal piety was not matched by his political competency. He was nearly always dominated by someone: his wife Eudokia, his formidable sister Pulcheria, the court eunuch Chrysaphius, the master of the offices Nonus, or the pillar-saint Simeon Stylites. He summoned the council of Ephesus in 431 (see n. 85 below), but fell off his horse and died the year before Chalcedon. He was the son of Arcadius (see n. 53 below) and the grandson of Theodosius I (*ibid.*).

50. Although the Senate of Constantinople was the descendant of the old Roman Senate, its powers and privileges were very different. It consisted, says Stephen Runciman, 'of all present and past holders of offices and rank above a certain level and their descendants. It was thus a vast amorphous body comprising everyone of prominence, of wealth and of a respectable position in the Empire' (*Byzantine Civilization* [London, 1933] 72). See further, *ibid.* 72-74.

51. Antinōou is Antinoë or Antinoupolis, the city founded by Hadrian in 130 c.e. in honour of his handsome favourite Antinous. In its day it was a fine town, but little now remains. The ruins lie to the east of the modern village of Esh-Sheik 'Ibâda a few miles from Mallawi/Mellawi, and it is more than a hundred miles downstream from the White Monastery. See further Amélineau, *Géographie* 48-51.

52. There is a brief lacuna in the manuscript here.
53. Arcadius and Honorius were the two sons of Theodosius I (Theodosius the Great), who was emperor from 379 to 395. On his death he left the eastern part of the empire to the weak and irritable Arcadius (383-408), and the west to the equally feeble Honorius (393-423). Honorius died without issue, but Arcadius produced Theodosius II (see n. 49 above).
54. The term is Greek (*proestōs*) and refers to the superior of a monastic community.
55. Šiēt is Scetis or the Wadi'n-Natrûn,' the heart of Egyptian monasticism. It lies far to the north, deep in the desert between Alexandria and Cairo. The Syriac version of the *Vita* published by Nau reads here: 'Some monks from the monastery of the holy and illustrious apa Macarius . . . ' , and it was this monastery which was the first to be established in Scetis.
56. Antony the Great (250?-356) was the real founder of anchoritic, as distinct from coenobitic, monasticism. He was born in Middle Egypt of Christian parents who died when he was eighteen. Some six months after their death he heard Mt 19:21 read in the liturgy ('If you would be perfect, go, sell what you possess and give to the poor'), and this is precisely what Antony did. For about fifteen years he practised the ascetic life near his old home, but when he found that his solitude was being disturbed by more and more visitors, he crossed the Nile and retired to the 'Outer Mountain' at Pispir where, for the next twenty years, he lived in an abandoned fort. His example stimulated many to imitate him, and in the early years of the third century there appeared in Egypt large numbers of ascetics, all of whom looked to Antony as their spiritual father. He himself remained a hermit for most of his life and died in 356 at the age, we are told, of one hundred and five. His biography was written by Athanasius the Great and there are at least six English translations: the earliest was produced in 1697 and the most recent in 1980. Antony is commemorated in the Coptic church on 22nd Tybi = 17 January.
57. Cyril of Alexandria (see n. 21 above), who is mentioned by name in Nau's Syriac version.
58. Most writers seem agreed that this story is a fairy-tale re-telling of a rather more prosaic event. What actually seems to have happened, and what Shenoute himself says happened in one of his letters, is as follows. Because of his continual violence, our hero had once again brought himself to the unfavourable notice of the authorities, and the local magistrate and one of his

assistants came to the monastery to see what could be done. A scuffle developed in which Shenoute grabbed the magistrate by his chain of office and said to him: 'Who are you? . . . If you are a spirit or angel who comes from God, I, too, am his servant; but if you have ceased [to serve him], I certainly will not cease!' At which point, Shenoute hurled his opponent to the ground and trampled over him. It was this event, according to E. Revillout ('Les origines du schisme égyptien; premier récit: le précurseur et inspirateur Sénuti le prophète' in *Revue de l'histoire des religions* 8 [1883] 415). P. Ladeuze (*Étude sur le cénobitisme Pakhomien pendant le IVᵉ siècle et la première moitié du Vᵉ* [Louvain, 1898; rpt. Frankfurt am Main, 1961] 138-139), Amélineau (*Vie de Schnoudi* 144-145, 153-154), and Leipoldt (*Schenute* 151), which lies at the basis of the story narrated by Besa. For the text of Shenoute's letter, see CSCO 42 (Copt. 2) 37-41.

59. Martyrius was archimandrite of Phbōou, the second major Pachomian foundation (see *Vita* 93), but little is known of him and he is not commemorated in the *Synaxarium*. Phbōou, the modern Fâw, is about sixty miles up the river from the White Monastery (see Amélineau, *Géographie* 331-333).

60. The text is corrupt here, and my translation follows Lefort's emendation as given in Wiesmann's Latin translation (see the bibliography at the end of this volume) 20 n. 2.

61. *Lit.* 'he went up' (*afi epšōi* [B]), which is how one gets out of a boat in Coptic. This is the only indication in this story that the preceding conversation has taken place aboard a vessel. Nau's Syriac version is rather different: after John has said 'He does not even know what he ate yesterday [Coptic: this evening]', the text continues: '[Apa Martyrius] did not listen, but went on to the monastery of apa Shenoute . . . '. We might add that this is not the only variant to appear in the Syriac version of this episode: Shenoute's speech to John is also somewhat different. And to add further confusion, the Arabic *Life* contains material which appears neither in the Syriac nor the Coptic.

62. See n. 50 above.

63. Amélineau has identified Pleuit with the village of Banâwît/ Banwaît, situated on the west bank of the Nile about fifteen miles north of Sohâg and about a dozen miles from the White Monastery (see Amélineau, *Géographie* 359-360). On the events at Pleuit, see further CSCO 42 (Copt. 2) 84-90.

64. We cannot now locate the island of Panehēou since Shenoute

sank it, and all we can say (with Besa) is that it was opposite Akhmîm. The Arabic *Life* translates the name as 'island of the wind', but this is certainly incorrect. Amélineau suggests 'island of benefits' (*île des profits:* see his *Géographie* 299-300), but J. Černý prefers 'island of fields' (see his *Coptic Etymological Dictionary* [Cambridge, 1976] 349), a name which well agrees with Besa's description.

65. The Coptic text is not entirely clear here, and this is a loose translation to bring out what appears to be the sense. Wiesmann translates the passage more literally as '*sed bibere non pergent nisi ea quae hic sunt*' (p. 24 of Wiesmann's Latin translation). The Arabic *Life* records the saying rather differently, and Amélineau has suggested that the problem may lie with a misunderstanding on the part of the Bohairic translator (see p. 48 n. 11 of his French translation). Wine, we might add, though not normally forming part of an ascetic's diet, was required for a large number of feasts and commemorations, and there is nothing unusual in Shenoute's offering it in the circumstances related by Besa. See further Winlock/Crum, *Monastery of Epiphanius* 161-162 and D. J. Chitty, *The Desert a City* (Oxford, 1966; rpt. 1977) 44 n. 129.

66. The Blemmyes were a nomadic tribe of the eastern desert who, in alliance with the Nubians, harried Upper Egypt for decades. If, as seems likely, the invasion referred to here is the same as that mentioned below in *Vita* 106-108, it probably occurred in 450 when Maximus, the *dux Thebaidis* of the time (see n. 19 above), went out against them with Shenoute's blessing (see Ladeuze, *Étude sur le cénobitisme* 246-250 for a useful discussion). In the following year, the new emperor in Constantinople, Marcian, concluded a peace with the Blemmyes and thereby brought their predations to an end. See also *Vita* 137 below. For a full discussion of Shenoute's attitude to the Nubians and further historical detail, see J. Leipoldt, 'Berichte Schenutes über Einfälle der Nubier in Ägypten' in *Zeitschrift für aegyptische Sprache* 40 (1902-03) 126-140; 41 (1904) 148. Whether the Blemmyes actually released their prisoners because of Shenoute's dramatic interference (for it was certainly a common practice of Egyptian hermits to intercede for the release of prisoners: see Winlock/Crum, *Monastery of Epiphanius* 1:176 n. 4), or whether they found it politic to do so because their line of retreat was cut off by a neighbouring yet hostile tribe (see Milne, *History of Egypt Under Roman Rule* 99) is not a question with which we

need here concern ourselves.

67. The verb is *meletān* [G], which may mean reading, recitation, or meditation, and although we do come across cases where the term means 'meditation' in the commonly accepted sense (i.e. silent, interior reflection upon what one has heard read or preached), it normally refers to audible repetition of passages of scripture learned by heart. 'Meditation' in this sense, says Crum, 'is repeatedly prescribed in the Pachomian and the Sinuthian Rules and is to be practised on many occasions and during a variety of other occupations' (Winlock/Crum, *Monastery of Epiphanius* 166). For examples of the quantities of Scripture which had to be learned, see the Introduction to this translation, n. 79, and for a further brief discussion and further bibliographical references, see Veilleux, *Pachomian Koinonia I: 414.

68. See n. 59 above.

69. *Lit.* 'he is reciting my words piercingly' (*khenouthoux* [B]: see Crum, *Dictionary* 406-407 s.v. *tōks* [S]).

70. On the rules of Shenoute's monastery, see Ladeuze, *Étude sur le cénobitisme* 305-326 and Leipoldt, *Schenute* 99-106. The latter's discussion is still very useful, though now in need of some revision. As Crum points out, 'a "rule", in the precise monastic sense, does not appear to have been formulated; at any rate not by Shenoute, nor, I believe, by his predecessor' ('A Study in the History of Egyptian Monasticism' 131), and what we are dealing with is a series of letters or 'canons' (Shenoute's term, as well as Besa's: see Leipoldt, *Schenute* 102-103 and A. A. Schiller, '*Kanōn* and *Kanōnize* in the Coptic Texts' in *Coptic Studies in Honor of Walter Ewing Crum* [Boston, 1950] 175-184). These 'canons' of Shenoute were based on those of Pachomius, but, like those of Pjol, they were considerably more detailed and considerably more rigorous (see Leipoldt, *Schenute* 48-49, 102, 117).

71. This is about the only piece of evidence we have that the Eucharist was celebrated at the White Monastery at least once a week. In the Pachomian monasteries it was celebrated twice a week, on Saturday evening and Sunday morning (see J. Muyser, 'Le Samedi et le Dimanche dans l'église et la littérature copte' in T. Mina, *Le martyre d'apa Epima* [Cairo, 1937] 89-111), but we have no information as to whether or not this was the case in Shenoute's cloister.

72. 'House-master' = *rmnēi* [B], which means literally 'man of the house'. Crum (*Dictionary* 66b) prefers 'monastic superintendent'

or 'warden'. In a classic Pachomian monastery, each house within the enclosing wall of the *koinōnia* might hold between twenty and forty monks, and each house had its own house-master and second (see n. 83 below). For a brief discussion, see Chitty, *The Desert a City* 22, 25-26.

73. The annual inundation of the Nile, God's 'yearly mercy' according to Shenoute (see Crum, *Dictionary* 197b), was the only thing that kept Egypt habitable. Without it, the country would simply have returned to the desert. In the neighbourhood of Akhmîm, the Nile would begin to rise in late May or early June and reach its maximum height about the end of the first week of September. As the waters subsided, crops would be sown on the rich and fertile mud-flats left uncovered, and harvested the following April and May.

74. See n. 66 above.

75. This, says Lefort, is very curious, since no such practice has ever been recorded among the monastic communities of Upper Egypt. He suggests, therefore, that instead of reading *oeik* [S]; *ōik* [B] 'bread', we read *oeik* [S] 'reeds, rushes', so that what were laid out were not loaves, but reeds to be dried for making ropes, mats, baskets, etc. (see Lefort's note in Wiesmann's Latin translation of the *Vita*, 30 n. 2). Rope and basket-making were the characteristic occupations of Egyptian ascetics and appear constantly in the literature (see Winlock/Crum, *Monastery of Epiphanius* 115 and Chitty, *The Desert a City* 3, 40 n. 35). Amélineau, however, has a different view, and suggests that it was the dough, not the finished bread, which was being put out to rise in the sun, and adds that it would have been about nine or ten o'clock in the morning, 'for that is the time at which I have seen this operation carried out' (*Vie de Schnoudi* 141 n. 1; see also p. 61 n. 8 of his French translation of the *Vita*). On the other hand, if Besa had wanted to say 'dough', he could have done so (the word is *ouōšm* [SB]), and I remain uncertain as to which of these views to accept.

76. *Lit.* 'a month of days'. See n. 46 above.

77. *Lit.* 'the great sons'. This could refer either to the older and senior brothers as distinct from the novices (see n. 29 above), or to the members of the administrative hierarchy of the monastery. There would, of course, be an overlap between the two, but I think 'senior brothers' is probably the more accurate rendering here. In *Vita* 173, therefore, the phrase which I have translated as 'both small and great' could also mean more specifically 'both the novices and the senior brethren'. For the house-master,

see n. 72 above.

78. *Lit.* 'they were not changed to life'.

79. John the Carpenter is the famous John of Lycopolis/Asyût. Born of devout christian parents, he went to Scetis when he was twenty-five, and lived the ascetic life there for some years before returning to his native Lycopolis. The monks of one of the local monasteries built him a three-chambered cell on the cliff-face of a mountain east of the city and brought him his food when he needed it and, as Besa tells us, he would speak with those who came to see him through a little window. Even this, we might add, was restricted, for the monks who guarded the way to his eyrie would let visitors pass only on Saturdays and Sundays. Shenoute visited him many times, and during his lifetime he acquired a great reputation not only as a holy man, but also as a prophet. He lived as a solitary for more than forty years and died in 394. Of all the friends and companions of Shenoute mentioned in the *Vita,* he is the only one to appear in the *Historia monachorum in Aegypto* (see the Introduction to this translation, nn. 43-44), and he is commemorated in the Coptic *Synaxarium* on 21st Athor (*hatōr* [S]; *athōr* [B]) = 17th November (see O'Leary, *Saints of Egypt* 169-170).

80. *Lit.* 'little place'. A 'cell' is actually *ri* [SB], as in *Vita* 122 (for a brief discussion of this term and its use, see Winlock/Crum, *Monastery of Epiphanius* 128).

81. This is what the text says, but we are probably to understand 'beside the road'.

82. See n. 73 above.

83. A *deutolarios* [SB] / *deuterarios* [G], 'second', in the classic Pachomian system could refer either to the assistant to a house-master (see n. 72 above), or to the second-in-command of a monastery as a whole. Theodore, for example, was 'second' to Pachomius in his administration of all the monasteries. If we were to translate *Vita* 123 into Western terms, Shenoute would be the abbot, and his 'second' would be the prior. See further Veilleux, *Pachomian Koinonia I:* 413 and Lampe, *Patristic Greek Lexicon* s.v. '*deuterarios*'.

84. If this is the same Gesios whom we met earlier (*Vita* 88), it will be remembered that he came to a bad end.

85. This synod is the council of Ephesus, the third Ecumenical Council, summoned by Theodosius II (see n. 49 above) in 431. The history of the council is far from elevating, and even if Shenoute's violent attack on Nestorius never really occurred

(see the Introduction to this study, n. 99), Besa's tale (which he obviously tells with approval) may well reflect the sort of negotiations which actually took place. Cyril of Alexandria (see n. 21 above) opened the council on 22 June 431 without waiting either for John of Antioch and the Syrian bishops (who were likely to support Nestorius) or for the papal legates. It is no surprize, then, that as a consequence of this wholly biased council, 'the impious Nestorius' was excommunicated and his doctrines condemned. The Greek *Acta* of this council are of considerable value; the Coptic *Acta* are not.

86. The *oularion* [B] is not the *velarium* [L] as Wiesmann suggests (in his Latin translation of the *Vita*, 57), but the *orarion* [G] / *orarium* [L], the stole which is now worn by deacons in the Orthodox church. For details of its nature and use in the Coptic church—a more complex matter than in the Greek—see Butler, *Ancient Coptic Churches of Egypt* 2:127-143.

87. *Oukouji nalou* [B]. As O'Leary points out, 'in reading the lives of Egyptian ascetes we are often surprised at the tender age at which a candidate was admitted to the monastic life. In many cases the monasteries were recruited by the system of "oblates", that is of children, sometimes not more than infants, who were given to the monastery to be brought up as monks . . . . [These *oblati*] became inmates of the monastery itself, and the presence of this youthful element was the cause of much noise, disorder, and mischief' (*Saints of Egypt* 253-254). The mischief, we might add, was not always good, clean fun: the desert fathers were well aware that the presence of these youngsters could easily lead to homosexuality (see Chitty, *The Desert a City* 66-67). See further Winlock/Crum, *Monastery of Epiphanius* 139, where the case of a three-year-old oblate is recorded.

88. The term is *komēs* [GSB] = *comes* [L]. Constantine was the first to establish *comes* as an official title and to classify it into three grades: *ordinis primi, secundi,* and *tertii.* The *comes* referred to here, however, is the *comes Aegypti* or *comes rei militaris* of Egypt (a title which appeared only after Constantine's death), and he occupied one of the most senior and influential administrative positions in Egypt. The two *duces* (see n. 19 above) were subordinate to the *comes,* though at an earlier period the distinction between them was somewhat blurred. For further information on this complex matter, see Jones, *Later Roman Empire* Index s.v. '*comes*'.

89. This is a loose translation to bring out the sense.

90. *Oikonomos* [GSB]. The *oikonomos* or 'steward' seems to have been in charge of the overall practical day-to-day running of the monastery, but his precise relationship to the abbot, second, and house-masters is not altogether clear. In the Pachomian texts, we find some overlapping of functions and titles, and exactly who is what can sometimes only be determined from the context. Cf. Veilleux' comment on the difficulties of *Vita Prima Graeca* 54 in his *Pachomian Koinonia I:* 413.

91. In Coptic, *toou* [S] / *tōou* [B] may mean 'mountain', 'desert', 'community of ascetics', or 'cemetery', whichever seems applicable (see Crum, *Dictionary* 440b-441b). Its original meaning (Middle Egyptian *dw*) was only 'mountain'. A similar episode to that related in *Vita* 154 ff. is to be found in the Life of Pijimi (see O'Leary, *Saints of Egypt* 231-232, for an account of this ascetic), and reads as follows: 'After [abba Shenoute] left his monastery, he neither ate nor drank on his journey. Pijimi said to him, "Take this jar and fill it with water from the stream to the east", and he took the vessel and filled it with water. When he came up, he found the old man standing and praying to God. When he went into the cell he found the pot on the ground boiling what was to be cooked. Then abba Shenoute realized in his heart that it was abba Pijimi whose throne and crown had been shown to him.

'When they had prayed together, they ate the small amount of cooked [food] and rested. In the middle of the night they arose and worshipped together, and spent the whole night praising God and singing spiritual songs.

'After these things, abba Shenoute [told abba Pijimi about the] marvel [concerning] his throne [and] his crown. When these things had happened, they went out . . . walking in the fields with . . . God willed that in this way the election of abba Shenoute should be revealed to abba Pijimi.

'It happened that as the two of them were walking, they came upon a corpse buried in that place, for truly, there were many bodies of the pagans of old buried there. Abba Shenoute was walking along with the little palm-branch in his hand, [and came] upon a dead man's skull. Abba Shenoute struck the skull three times and the corpse immediately opened [its mouth?] and spoke with abba Shenoute and abba Pijimi like this: "Hail! Hail, true worshippers of Christ and servants of the most high God! [Great?] grace has come upon me in death, for your . . . . For behold, from now on [I] shall . . . ' .

The text then breaks off, but we know what happened because the story parallels a similar incident in the life of Macarius the Great, and we may read the whole tale in *The Sayings of the Desert Fathers: The Alphabetical Collection,* tr. Benedicta Ward (CS 59; Kalamazoo, 1975) 115-116. The Coptic text of this fragment of the *Life of Pijimi* may be found (with minor variations) in Evelyn White, *Monasteries of the Wadi'n-Natrûn* 1:162 or CSCO 41 (Copt. 1) 77-78.

92. Šmoun is the Greek Hermopolis and the modern El-Ashmûnein. It is just opposite Antinoë (see n. 51 above) on the other bank of the river (see further Amélineau, *Géographie* 167-170). According to Amélineau, Wiesmann, and the Arabic *Life,* Šmoun here should be amended to Šmin, and, as a consequence, 'go north' at n. 93 below should be changed to 'go south'. I cannot agree with this. Coptic tradition asserts that when the Holy Family fled to Egypt, they certainly stayed for a while in Šmoun (where the child Jesus, we are told, healed crowds of sick people and performed other miracles), and then travelled south to Mallawi and eventually to El-Qûsîya. Here they stayed for six months in the Dair al-Muharraq, which is still a very important Coptic monastery, and then, according to an oral tradition, went further south to Asyût before returning to Dair al-Muharraq. In other words, the most southerly place they visited in Egypt was Asyût, and Asyût is some sixty miles *north* of Šmin / Akhmîm (for details of all these traditions, see Meinardus, *Christian Egypt: Ancient and Modern* 601-649, and M. Jullien, 'Traditions et légendes coptes sur le voyage de la Sainte-Famille en Égypte', *Les missions catholiques* 19 [1887] 9-12, 20-24). Since I know of no surviving tradition which has the Holy Family visiting Šmin, I see no need to make any change in Besa's text.

93. If Šmoun can remain Šmoun, north can remain north: see n. 92 above.

94. *Lit.* 'because of the amount of its fruit'.

95. *Lit.* 'the gourd went backwards'. The same expression occurs in the first sentence of *Vita* 170.

96. See n. 77 above.

97. 1st Epiphi = 25th June.

98. 6th Epiphi = 30th June.

99. *Mpn* in Leipoldt's text is a typographical error for *mēn*, the qualitative form of *moun* [SB] 'remain, continue, persevere'.

100. 7th Epiphi = 1st July.

101. *Lit.* 'according to your choir (*choros* [G])'.

102. Which apa Pšoi is Shenoute invoking? Is it apa Pšoi from Mount
   Psōou, the traditional founder of the Red Monastery (see n. 14
   above)? We know that the latter 'composed many admonitions
   and instructions for monks and laity' (see *ibid.*: none of these has
   survived), but we have no evidence that Shenoute ever looked to
   him as a spiritual father, and it would perhaps be a little unusual
   to find him in such elevated and distinguished company as
   Antony and Pachomius. It may be then that Shenoute is calling
   on the much more famous apa Pšoi who was the friend of Paul of
   Tamwah and one of the early settlers in Scetis. This Pšoi was
   a companion of John Colobos/John the Little/John the Dwarf,
   and both were originally associated with the two monasteries
   founded in Scetis by Macarius the Great. Both then moved
   away from these monasteries and organized their own founda-
   tions, thus establishing the four ancient monasteries of Scetis.
   When Scetis was raided by the Berbers in 407/408, Pšoi fled for
   refuge to a mountain near Antinoë (see n. 51 above) where he
   met Paul of Tamwah. The two became devoted friends, and
   according to Coptic tradition they could not be separated even
   in death. When Pšoi's relics were being transported to the
   monastery of St Shenoute in Antinoë soon after he died, the
   boat refused to move until the relics of Paul had also been
   brought aboard. Both were then taken to Antinoë, and there
   they remained until the ninth century. At that time, they were
   again translated back to Pšoi's own foundation at Scetis, and
   there (together with the relics of Ephraem the Syrian) they still
   remain. Pšoi's feast-day is the day following that of Shenoute:
   8th Epiphi = 2nd July. See further O'Leary, *Saints of Egypt*
   106-107 and O.F.A. Meinardus, *Christian Egypt: Faith and Life*
   (Cairo, 1970) 156-157. For bibliographical information on
   *vitae* of Pšoi in Greek, Syriac, and Arabic, see Chitty, *The Desert
   a City* 78 n. 40.
103. For Antony, see n. 56 above.
104. Pachomius was the founder of coenobitic monasticism. He seems
   to have been born about 292 in Upper Egypt and to have been
   conscripted into the army under Constantine. When he was
   released (or when he escaped) from the army he spent some three
   years with the ascetic and hermit Palaemon. Then, in about 320,
   he founded the community of Tabennesi near Akhmîm, the first
   Pachomian foundation, and large numbers of monks flocked to
   him, attracted by his sanctity and his charisma. Other communities soon followed, and by the time of Pachomius' death in

about 346 c.e., there were nine monasteries for men and two for women under his administration. Both the organization and the rule of these communities were the models for those of the White Monastery. Pachomius is commemorated in the Coptic *Synaxarium* on 14th Bashons (*pašons* [SB] ; *pachōn* [B] ) = 9th May, and is the subject of a large number of *Lives:* see the monumental work of Veilleux, *Pachomian Koinonia,* three volumes, for a translation of the entire Pachomian *corpus,* and *ibid.* 1: 477-488 for a detailed bibliography.

105. *Oukapsa esoi ncholchol* [B]: the *kapsa* [G] is certainly a chest, but what *esoi ncholchol* means is not at all clear. Wiesmann (45) suggests *in arca ornata,* and Amélineau (91) 'une châsse percée de trous', but neither of these is certain. *Kolkl* [S] seems to be derived from the Semitic *galgal* 'wheel' (see Černý, *Coptic Etymological Dictionary* 55) and may mean 'round' or 'curved' (see Crum, *Dictionary* 103a), but it is not easy to see how this could be applied to Shenoute's coffin. W. Erichsen's *Demotisches Glossar* (Copenhagen, 1954) offers no real assistance, for promising roots such as *ḥl* 'to shine, gleam, be splendid, brightness, splendour, lustre' (see *ibid.* 368) cannot be forced into *cholchol* without insurmountable linguistic difficulties.

106. On the burial customs of the Egyptian monks, see Winlock/Crum, *Monastery of Epiphanius* 1:183-185 (and Plates XI and XII), and Walters, *Monastic Archaeology* 229-236.

# BIBLIOGRAPHY

*Abbreviations*

BIFAO  *Bulletin de l'Institut français d'archéologie orientale*
CSCO   *Corpus Scriptorum Christianorum Orientalium*
JTS    *Journal of Theological Studies*
ZAS    *Zeitschrift für aegyptische Sprache*

A.  EDITIONS AND TRANSLATIONS OF BESA'S
    LIFE OF SHENOUTE
    1   *The Bohairic Life*
        J. Leipoldt and W. E. Crum, *Sinuthii Archimandritae Vita et Opera Omnia*, CSCO 41 (Copt. 1) 1906. Bohairic text.
        *Ibid.*, CSCO 129 (Copt. 16) 1951. Latin translation by H. Wiesmann, completed by L. T. Lefort.
        E. C. Amélineau, *Monuments pour servir à l'histoire de l'Égypte chrétienne aux IV^e, V^e, VI^e et VII^e siècles (Mission archéologique française au Caire, Mémoires 4).* Paris, 1888-1895 1:1-91. Bohairic text and French translation.
    2   *The Sahidic Fragments*
        These have been collected by Amélineau in *Monuments* 1:237-246 (and see also *ibid.* 2:633 ff.). A further fragment was published by Urbain Bouriant in 'Fragments de manuscrits thébains du Musée de Boulaq', *Recueil de travaux relatifs à la philologie et à l'archéologie égyptiennes* 4 (1883) 1-4, 152-156.
    3   *The Arabic Life*
        Amélineau, *Monuments* 1:289-478. Arabic text and French translation.
    4   *The Syriac Lives*
        F. N. Nau, 'Une version syriaque inédite de la Vie de Schenoudi', *Revue sémitique d'epigraphie et d'histoire*

ancienne 7 (1899) 356-363; 8 (1900) 153-167, 252-265.
The sole fragment of the other Syriac *Life* was published by
I. Guidi in the *Gesellschaft der Wissenschaften zu Göttin-
gen. Nachrichten* 3 (1889) 46-56.

B.    EDITIONS AND TRANSLATIONS OF BESA'S WORKS
K. H. Kuhn, *Letters and Sermons of Besa*, CSCO 157-158
(1956). Coptic text and English translation.

C.    EDITIONS AND TRANSLATIONS OF SHENOUTE'S WORKS
There have been only two attempts at a complete edition of
Shenoute's works:
E. C. Amélineau, *Oeuvres de Schenoudi*. Paris, 1907-1914.
Two volumes. Coptic text and French translation.
Leipoldt/Crum, *Sinuthii Archimandritae Vita et Opera Omnia*,
CSCO 42 (Copt. 2) 1908, and CSCO 73 (Copt. 5) 1913.
Coptic text. *Ibid.*, CSCO 96 (Copt. 8) 1931, and CSCO
108 (Copt. 12) 1936. Latin translations by H. Wiesmann of
CSCO 42 and CSCO 73 respectively.
The edition of Leipoldt and Crum is much superior to that of
Amélineau (see F. N. Nau, 'A propos d'une édition des oeuvres
de Schenoudi: la version syriaque des prières de Schenoudi, de
Jean le Nain, de Macaire l'égyptien et de Sérapion', *Revue de
l'orient chrétien* 12 [1907] 313-328 for a critical review of the
latter's work), but neither edition is actually complete. That of
Amélineau contains more texts than that of Leipoldt and Crum,
but there are substantial amounts of Shenoutian works to be
found in manuscripts at present in Paris, Vienna, Cairo, Michigan,
London, Manchester, Oxford, and Cambridge. The editions of
Amélineau and Leipoldt/Crum must therefore be supplemented
by the work of such scholars as du Bourguet, Chassinat, Guérin,
Hyvernat, Koschorke, Lefort, Shisha-Halevy, and Teza, whose
studies are listed in Section E of this Bibliography.
There are reviews of the Leipoldt/Crum edition by H. Junker
in *Deutsche morgenländische Gesellschaft. Zeitschrift* 67 (1913)
187, by W. Spiegelberg in *Orientalistische Literaturzeitung* 12
(1909) 439-441, 17 (1914) 505-506, and by G. Maspero in
*Revue critique d'histoire et de littérature* (1906) 442.

D.    EDITIONS AND TRANSLATIONS OF PSEUDO-SHENOUTE
According to Ariel Shisha-Halevy, this interesting text 'represents
a stratifiable mixture of distinct Shenoutian and extraneous elements, rather than a homogeneous non-Shenoutian text simply
and falsely attributed to Shenoute' (A. Shisha-Halevy, 'Two New
Shenoute-Texts from the British Library', *Orientalia* 44 [1975]
151 n. 13).

K. H. Kuhn, *Pseudo-Shenoute on Christian Behaviour,* CSCO 206 (Copt. 29) 1960.

E. TEXTS AND STUDIES ON SHENOUTE AND BESA
This bibliography lists only those studies which are devoted either entirely or almost entirely to Shenoute and Besa.

Amélineau, E. C. *Les moines égyptiens: Vie de Schnoudi* (Paris, 1889).

Barns, J. 'Shenute as a Historical Source', *Actes du Xe congrès international de papyrologues, Varsovie-Cracovie 3-9 septembre 1961* (Wroclaw, 1964) 151-159.

Benigni, U. *'Didachê Coptica:* "Duarum Viarum" Recensio Coptica Monastica, Shenudii Homiliis Attributa, per Arabicam Versionem Superstes', *Bessarione* 4 (1898-99) 311-329.

Bethune-Baker, J. F. 'The Date of the Death of Nestorius: Schenute, Zacharias, Evagrius', JTS O.S. 9 (1908) 601-605.

du Bourguet, P. 'Entretien de Chenouté sur les devoirs des juges', BIFAO 55 (1956) 85-109.

————. 'Entretien de Chenouté sur des problèmes de discipline ecclésiastique et de cosmologie', BIFAO 57 (1958) 99-104.

————. 'Diatribe de Chenouté contre le démon', *Société d'archéologie copte. Bulletin* 16 (1961-62) 17-72.

Buckle, D. P. 'A Noteworthy Sahidic Variant in a Shenoute Homily in the John Rylands Library', *Bulletin of the John Rylands Library* 20 (1936) 383-384.

Burmester, O. H. E. 'The Homilies or Exhortations of the Holy Week Lectionary', *Le Muséon* 45 (1932) 21-70.

Chassinat, E. *Le quatrième livre des entretiens et epîtres de Shenouti (Institut français d'archéologie orientale. Mémoires* 23) Cairo, 1911.

Crum, W. E. 'Inscriptions from Shenoute's Monastery', JTS O.S. 5 (1904) 552-569.

Erichsen, W. 'Ein Sendbrief eines ägyptischen Klostervorstehers', *Jahrbuch für das Bistum Mainz* 5 (1950) 310-313.

Erman, A. 'Schenute und Aristophanes', ZÄS 32 (1894) 134-135.

Galtier, E. 'Note sur une homélie de Schenouti', BIFAO 6 (1908) 179.

Garitte, G. 'A propos des lettres de saint Antoine l'ermite', *Le Muséon* 52 (1939) 11-31.

Gaselee, S. 'Hymnus de Sinuthio', in S. Gaselee, *Parerga Coptica III* (Cambridge, 1912-14).

————. 'Hymni duo de Sinuthio', *Le Muséon* 33 (1915) 116-118.

Grohmann, A. 'Die im äthiopischen, arabischen und koptischen erhaltenen Visionen Apa Schenutes von Atripe', *Deutsche Morgenländische Gesellschaft. Zeitschrift* 67 (1913) 187-267; 68 (1914) 1-46.

Guérin, H. 'Sermons inédits de Senouti', *Revue égyptologique* 10 (1902) 148-164; 11 (1904) 15-34.

Hyvernat, H. *Bibliothecae Pierpont Morgan Codices Coptici Photographice Expressi, Vol. 54: Sinuthii Archimandritae de Ecclesia Frequentanda Sermo,* Rome, 1922.

Koschorke, K. *et al.* 'Schenute: De Certamine Contra Diabolum', *Oriens Christianus* 59 (1975) 60-77.

Kuhn, K. H. 'Besa's Letters and Sermons', *Le Muséon* 66 (1953) 225-243.

————. 'A Fifth-Century Egyptian Abbot', JTS 5 (1954) 36-48 ('Besa and His Background'); 5 (1954) 174-187 ('Monastic Life in Besa's Day'); 6 (1955) 35-48 ('Besa's Christianity').

————. 'The Observance of the "Two Weeks" in Shenoute's Writings', in *Studia Patristica 2* (Berlin, 1957) 427-434.

————. 'Pseudo-Shenoute on Christian Behaviour', *Le Muséon* 71 (1958) 359-380.

van Lantschoot, A. 'A propos du *Physiologus*', in *Coptic Studies in Honor of W. E. Crum* (Boston, 1950) 339-363.

Lefort, L. T. 'Athanase, Ambroise, et Chenouté "Sur la virginité",' *Le Muséon* 48 (1935) 55-73.

————. 'Un passage obscur des hymnes à Chenouté', *Orientalia* 4 (1935) 411-415.

————. 'La chasse aux reliques des martyrs en Égypte au IVe siècle', *La nouvelle Clio* 6 (1954) 225-230.

————. 'Catéchèse christologique de Chenouté', ZAS 80 (1955) 40-45.

Leipoldt, J. *Schenute, der Begründer der national ägyptischen Kirche* (Diss., Leipzig, 1903).

————. *Schenute von Atripe und die Entstehung des national ägyptischen Christentums (Texte und Untersuchungen* 25, 1) Leipzig, 1903.

————— . 'Berichte Schenutes über Einfälle der Nubier in Ägypten', ZAS 40 (1902-03) 126-140; 41 (1904) 148. There were some inaccuracies in this important article which were pointed out by O. E. von Lemm in his *Kleine Koptische Studien* 45 (see below, s.v. von Lemm, O. E.) 0219-0223.

————— . 'Ein bohairisches Lied zum Preise Schenutes', ZAS 43 (1906) 152-156.

————— . 'Ein Kloster lindert Kriegsnot. Schenûtes Bericht über die Tätigkeit des Weissen Klosters bei Sohag', in ' . . . *und fragten nach Jesus': Festschrift für E. Barnikol zum 70. Geburtstag* (Berlin, 1964) 52-56.

von Lemm, O. E. *Kleine Koptische Studien XLV: Bemerkungen zu einigen Werken des Schenute* (*Bulletin de l'Académie Impériale des Sciences de Saint-Pétersbourg* 21/3) St Petersburg/Leningrad, 1904.

Lucchesi, E. *Étude du nom dans la langue copte de Schenoute* (Diss., *pro manuscripto*; Université de Fribourg, 1973).

Monneret de Villard, U. 'La fondazione del Deyr el-Abiad', *Aegyptus* 4 (1923) 156-162.

Quecke, H. 'Zu Schenutes Gebrauch des Qualitativs', *Orientalia Lovaniensia Periodica* 6-7 (1975-76) 479-486.

Revillout, E. 'Les origines du schisme égyptien; premier récit: le précurseur et inspirateur Sénuti le prophète', *Revue de l'histoire des religions* 8 (1883) 401-467, 545-581.

Shisha-Halevy, A. 'Unpublished Shenoutiana in the British Library', *Enchoria* 5 (1975) 53-108.

————— . 'Commentary on Unpublished Shenoutiana in the British Library', *Enchoria* 6 (1976) 29-61.

————— . 'Two New Shenoute-Texts from the British Library', *Orientalia* 44 (1975) 149-185, 469-484.

————— . 'Akhmîmoid Features in Shenoute's Idiolect', *Le Muséon* 89 (1976) 353-366.

Teza, E. 'Frammenti inediti di un sermone di Scenuti in dialetto Sahidico', *Accademia nazionale dei Lincei. Classe di scienze morali. Rendiconti* Ser. 5, 1 (1892) 682-697.

Tisserant, E. 'Étude sur une traduction arabe d'un sermon de Chenoudi', *Revue de l'orient chrétien* 13 (1908) 81-89.

Thompson, H. 'Dioscorus and Shenoute', *École pratique des hautes études. Bibliothèque* 234 (1922) 367-376.

Treu, U. 'Aristophanes bei Schenute', *Philologus: Zeitschrift für das klassische Altertum* 101 (1957) 325-328.

Wiesmann, H. 'Zu zwei Schenute-Stellen', ZAS 62 (1927) 67.

Young, D. W. 'On Shenoute's Use of Present I'', *Journal of Near Eastern Studies* 20 (1961) 115-119.

————. 'Ešōpe and the Conditional Conjugation', *Journal of Near Eastern Studies* 21 (1962) 175-185.

————. 'Unfulfilled Conditions in Shenoute's Dialect', *Journal of the American Oriental Society* 89 (1969) 399-407.

————. 'The Milieu of Nag Hammadi: Some Historical Considerations', *Vigilae Christianae* 24 (1970) 127-137.

# INDEX OF PROPER NAMES
*References are to paragraph numbers of the translation*